Out of the Nest

Cuckoo 2000

Nancy Allen

Nancy

Pat Glauser

Pat

Kay Bruce

Kay

Isla Reckling

Isla

Fran Fauntleroy

Fran

Mary Whilden

Mary

Our Special Thanks

We thank our families, extended families and friends for filling our nest with their tasty recipes.

Book coordination by Rita Mills
Cover and layout design by Mary Valle-Cooper, Yorké Design
Photography by Michael Martinez

We're back...still flappin' and squawkin'!

Our chicks have flown the coop and feathered

their own nests. We have wider waists, brighter hair,

and larger appetites...for life!

As we soar into 2000, this is our wish for you–

"May the road rise up to meet you

May the wind be always at your back

May the sun shine warm upon your face

May the rain fall softly upon your fields

And, until we meet again, may the Good Lord

hold you in the Hollow of His Hand."

Table of Contents

Appetizers & Drinks

Appetizers & Drinks

Preceding Page: The Allen Family
Top row–left to right: Eddie, Chinhui, Wilson & Randy.
Bottom row: Kendall, Nancy, Jessica, Janet, Jenny, Laurie, & Morgan.

John Luke's Queso

1	2-pound package Velveeta cheese	1	10-ounce can Rotel Tomatoes & Chilies, chopped
½	pound rat cheese	1	small white onion, grated
1	cup Monterrey Jack cheese	3-4	jalapeño peppers, chopped
1	pound sausage, ground		

Cook sausage until thoroughly browned. Drain all grease. Cut all the cheese into cubes. Put cheese in top of double boiler, & cook until melted. Add Rotel, onion, & peppers. Add browned sausage. Keep over hot water & serve with chips.

Note: This queso is delicious in an omelet. If the mixture is too thick, add more Rotel, plain tomatoes, or a little beer. The sausage can be omitted. An 8-ounce package of cream cheese may be added. Remove the seeds & membranes from the jalapeño peppers if you don't want the queso too spicy.

Caviar Pie

4	eggs, hard boiled & chopped (optional)	¾	cup sour cream
4	ounces cream cheese	2	tablespoons mayonnaise
1	stick butter	1	teaspoon lemon juice
½	medium size onion, grated	¼	teaspoon Worcestershire
1	bunch green onions, finely chopped	6	ounces caviar, black or red
			Dash Tabasco

Soften & cream together cream cheese & butter. Add chopped eggs, grated onion, lemon juice, seasonings & mayonnaise. Pat mixture into a circular mound onto a party tray. Cover with sour cream. Sprinkle green onions over top. Put in refrigerator. To serve, drain caviar & gently spoon over top of mound. Serve with Melba Toast or rounds.

Cheese Ball

3	12-ounce packages cream cheese		1	12-ounce package Swiss or Monterrey Jack cheese, grated
1	12-ounce package American cheese, grated		3	wedges blue cheese
1	12-ounce package mild Cheddar cheese, grated		3-6	garlic cloves, crushed
			1	onion, grated
			3	tablespoons chili powder

Soften cream cheese & add other cheeses. Mix well. Add garlic & onion & mix well. Roll into one or several balls. Roll ball in chili powder & serve with crackers.

Gary Hall's Cheese Wafers

Monterrey Jack Cheese   **Cayenne pepper**

Slice cheese into ¼" thick round slices, using a very small cookie cutter (slightly larger than a quarter). Place on a non-stick baking pan. Place pan in 375° oven in the center of rack. After a few minutes, the cheese will begin to bubble. When the bubbling stops, immediately take out of oven. Quickly remove cheese from pan with metal spatula & cool on wire rack. Sprinkle lightly with cayenne pepper. When room temperature, store in air tight container.

Note: Different brands of Monterrey Jack cheese have different amounts of fat content. If too much, the wafers will be chewy. Too little & they will crumble when taking them out of the pan. They should be crisp. Rice Epicurian Brand works best.

Rienzi Roasted Almonds

1	pound almonds, whole, blanched & skinless	Olive oil
		Salt, to taste

In a roasting pan, place almonds & enough olive oil to coat. Roast at 375°, stirring every few minutes until golden brown. Drain on paper towel. Sprinkle with salt. When at room temperature, store in an air tight container.

Note: If roasted until dark brown they will be bitter. Natural almonds are sometimes hard to find, but Jamails at Farmers Market & some Fiesta stores have them. Peanuts are also delicious done this way.

Salted Pecans

	White Karo Syrup	Salt
2½	pounds pecan halves	Large paper bag
½	stick butter, melted	

This recipe is my grandmother's and there is just one ingredient that makes it very special–white Karo syrup. In a 9x13" baking pan place carefully picked fresh pecan halves. Pour the melted butter over the pecans and toss gently until all nuts are coated. Place in preheated 400° oven for 12-14 minutes. Take out when brown. Watch pecans carefully as they tend to burn. While pecans are browning, tear open a large brown paper bag and lay it flat on the counter. Drizzle tiny streams of white Karo all over the paper bag. When the pecan halves are browned empty out onto the paper which you have just prepared with the white Karo syrup. Salt generously and toss with hands or spoon to make certain they are covered thoroughly with the salt. When room temperature, store in containers.

César's Famous Salsa

4	tomatoes, medium	4-6	cups of water	
3	jalapeños, more or less to taste		Salt & Pepper to taste	

Boil tomatoes and jalapeños until peppers change color. Drain almost all of the water, leave about a half cup in the pan. Throw everything in the blender. Blend at medium-low speed for 1-2 minutes. Add salt & pepper while blending. Do not over blend, try to keep the salsa chunky.

Doug's Hot Sauce

2	20-ounce cans of Pear Tomatoes, Italian Style	2	tablespoons salt
4	large cloves garlic, crushed	2	heaping tablespoons cilantro, finely chopped
2	tablespoons balsamic vinegar	6	large fresh jalapeños, deseeded & finely diced
2	tablespoons light vegetable oil	3	serrano peppers, finely diced

Drain the tomatoes and save the juice. Chop the tomatoes. Put the tomato juice and all the ingredients into a blender. Add the tomatoes last. Buzz for only 2 seconds.

Note: I recommend making at least 3 "batches" as it gets eaten quickly. Don't be tempted to use fresh tomatoes; the canned ones work better for this recipe. Flavor is best after sitting in the refrigerator overnight. Be sure to take the extra time to chop and dice the cilantro & jalapeños as finely as possible.

 # Robert's Easy Jalapeño Pie

Line pie plate with sliced jalapeño pepper slices. Add 10 ounces grated Cheddar cheese. Whip 4-6 eggs & pour over top. Bake 30-45 minutes at 350°. Serve with Mexican chips.

Baked Stuffed Shrimp Appetizer

12	jumbo shrimp, shelled & deveined		1	tablespoon finely chopped parsley
3	teaspoons extra virgin olive oil		1	teaspoon grated lemon zest
1	cup coarse bread crumbs		1	tablespoon fresh lemon juice
1	garlic clove, crushed through a press			

Preheat oven to 450°. Split shrimp along backs but not all the way through. Spray a baking pan with olive oil cooking spray. Arrange shrimp on pan. Heat 2 teaspoons of the olive oil in a large non-stick skillet. Add the bread crumbs and cook, stirring over medium low heat until the bread is golden. Add 1 tablespoon of the parsley, garlic and lemon zest, cook, stirring for 1 minute. Remove from heat. Carefully pack bread mixture into opening in each shrimp. Brush or drizzle each shrimp with remaining oil. Bake until shrimp are coated thoroughly about 5 minutes. Before serving, sprinkle with lemon juice.

New Caney Jalapeño Shrimp Sauce

1	8-ounce package cream cheese		1	jar New Caney Jalapeño Shrimp Sauce

Pour sauce over cream cheese. Delicious.

Note: Serve with crackers of your choice.

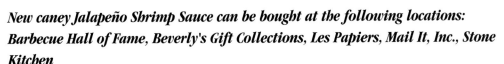

New caney Jalapeño Shrimp Sauce can be bought at the following locations: Barbecue Hall of Fame, Beverly's Gift Collections, Les Papiers, Mail It, Inc., Stone Kitchen

William's Cheese & Sausage Balls

3	cups Bisquick		1	pound ground pork sausage, uncooked
1	10-ounce block Sharp Cheddar cheese, grated			Cooking spray

Break up sausage with fork. Mix in Bisquick and grated cheese. Shape into round, bite-size balls (about 1-2" in size). Lightly grease baking sheet with cooking spray. Bake in preheated oven 350° until brown, about 20 minutes.

Grandma McFarren's Texas Niblets

2	9-ounce packages thin pretzel sticks		***Sauce:***	
1	12-ounce box Rice Chex		1	pound butter, melted
1	15-ounce box Wheat Chex		4	tablespoons Worcestershire
1	10-ounce box Cheerios		2	teaspoons celery salt
1	box Sunshine Cheese Crackers		1	cup cooking oil
½	pound pecans, browned in butter and salted		2	tablespoons Accent
			1½	teaspoons allspice
1	16-ounce can peanuts		1	teaspoon garlic powder
1	12-ounce can cashews		¼	teaspoon red pepper
3	6½-ounce cans mixed nuts			

Mix above ingredients in two large roaster pans (can use disposable).

Sauce: Mix above and pour over cereal and nut mixture evenly. Stir carefully. Bake at 250° for 1½ hours. Stir every 20 minutes while cooking. Cool before serving.

Shelley's Black Bean Dip

1	can black beans	4-5	stalks cilantro, chopped
1	red bell pepper, chopped	1	tablespoon sugar
1	yellow bell pepper, chopped	1	teaspoon cumin powder
2	jalapeño peppers, chopped	¾	cup lime juice

Mix all ingredients & chill for 2 hours. Serve with tortilla chips.

Shrimp Dip

1	pound large shrimp, peeled & cooked	½	cup mayonnaise
1	8-ounce package cream cheese	½	lemon, squeezed
½	cup green onions, chopped		Salt, pepper & garlic salt, to taste

Chop shrimp into really small pieces. Soften cream cheese & mix all ingredients together. Refrigerate before serving.

Fantastic Cheese Dip

1	pound Velveeta cheese, grated	1	4-ounce jar pimentos, sliced
1	pound sharp Cracker Barrel cheese, grated	1	4-ounce can green chilies, drained & chopped
1	pound Monterrey Jack cheese, grated	3	cloves garlic, crushed
1	quart Hellman's mayonnaise	3	whole jalapeño peppers, chopped fine
1	small onion, grated		

Place all ingredients in food processor & combine thoroughly. Add mayonnaise & mix well. Dip will keep in refrigerator up to 6 weeks. Onion, garlic & chilies should be adjusted to taste.

Randa's Corn Dip

1	8-ounce can corn, drained	1	14-ounce can green chiles, drained
1	cup sour cream	1	cup grated cheddar cheese
½	cup mayonnaise		Dash garlic salt
1	tablespoon chopped jalapeño		Salt & pepper to taste

Mix all ingredients together & chill overnight. Serve cold with crackers or chips.

Note: This dish can also be baked at 350° for 30 minutes to serve as a side dish.

Bryant's Bean Dip

2	15-ounce cans Trappey's Black Beans, drained & mashed	1	8-ounce jar Pace Thick & Chunky Picante Sauce
1	15-ounce can Trappey's black beans, whole	½	teaspoon salt
		½	teaspoon pepper
2	4-ounce cans green chiles, chopped	½	teaspoon garlic salt
		½	teaspoon Lawry's Salt
		2	cups Monterrey Jack cheese, grated

Combine all ingredients except the cheese. Bake in oven at 350° until hot and bubbly. Sprinkle Monterrey Jack cheese on top and it will melt by itself. Serve with tostados or Fritos.

Chunky Avocado Dip

4	tomatoes	2	tablespoons fresh cilantro
4	avocadoes	2	tablespoons oil
2	bunches green onions	⅓	cup red wine vinegar
1½	teaspoons salt		Pepper, to taste

Chop tomatoes, avocadoes, onions and cilantro very finely. Mix all ingredients together and refrigerate. Prepare ahead of time so dip can set at least 1 hour in the refrigerator. Serve with chips.

John's Cheese Dip

1	8-ounce package cream cheese	2	heaping tablespoons sour cream
½	lemon		Salt & pepper, to taste
2	tablespoons onion, grated		Dash of Tabasco
			Dash of Worchestershire

Soften cheese in microwave for 15 seconds. Combine all ingredients. Good served with any kind of chip or raw vegetable.

Note: For a Mexican taste, add 1 cup finely grated cheddar cheese and 3-4 tablespoons of picante sauce.

Inell's Deviled Eggs

6	eggs		Dash black pepper
2	tablespoons mayonnaise		Dash red pepper
1	tablespoon yellow mustard		Dash paprika
1½	tablespoons Durkees	¼	teaspoon salt

Boil eggs & let cool. Carefully peel, halve, and de-yolk. With electric beater, whip egg yolks with the remaining ingredients. Stuff into white halves, sprinkle tops with paprika & refrigerate.

Kim Bashaw's Cilantro Corn Dip

2	8-ounce packages cream cheese	3	dashes of Tabasco
¼	cup fresh lime juice	1	8-ounce can whole yellow corn
1	tablespoon cumin	1	cup pecans, chopped
1	teaspoon salt	3	tablespoons cilantro, chopped
1	teaspoon pepper	3	green onions, chopped
1	teaspoon cayenne pepper		Tortilla chips or blue corn chips
	Dash of lemon pepper		

Whip cream cheese until fluffy, then beat in lime juice, cumin, salt, pepper, cayenne, lemon pepper and Tabasco. Stir in corn, pecans, cilantro and green onions. Refrigerate. Serve with chips.

Aubrey Lynne's Mexicali Dip

1   3-ounce can pitted black olives, drained

1   4-ounce can chopped green chilies, drained

1   medium onion, chopped

1   large tomato, chopped

Mix ingredients with this dressing:

1½ tablespoons vinegar

3   tablespoons olive oil

1   teaspoon salt

Mix all and serve with tortilla chips.

Crab and Spinach Dip

2   packages frozen chopped spinach

1   pound fresh crab meat

1½ cups Sharp Cheddar Cheese, grated

1   cup green onions, finely chopped

1   can tomato paste

1   cup sour cream

    Salt & pepper, to taste

Thaw spinach and grate cheese. Layer spinach, onions, crab, cheese, and salt and pepper. Repeat once more. Refrigerate. When ready to bake, add sour cream and tomato paste on top. Bake 45 minutes in 325° oven. Serve with tortilla chips or toast points.

Scottie's Cocktail Cheese Balls

¼   pound butter

½   pound Sharp cheese, grated

1   cup flour

½   teaspoon salt

1   package onion soup mix

¼   cup parsley

Soften butter & cream with cheese. Add remaining ingredients & roll into bite-size balls. Bake at 400° for 5-10 minutes until golden brown. Yields about 90 balls. May be frozen before baking.

Aunt Mary's Paté Maison

½ pound lean ham, cut into ½" chunks
½ pound veal, chicken or turkey, cut into ½" chunks
½ pound bacon, cut into ½" pieces
1 clove garlic, cut in half

Salt & pepper, to taste
1 egg
Pinch ground cinnamon
1 tablespoon Cognac or other good brandy
1 bay leaf, place on top not in blender

Process in blender all ingredients until minced or finely chopped. Put in loaf pan, packing firmly. Press bay leaf into meat mixture. Bake uncovered, until pate has pulled away from side of pan & is nicely browned, about 45 minutes in a preheated 400° oven. Cool & refrigerate for 1 day before slicing & serving.

Note: A well seasoned meat loaf to be eaten cold. Keeps in refrigerator 4-5 days.

Green Lizards

1 12-ounce can Minute Maid Limeade
10-12 ounces Vodka

4-5 sprigs mint, fresh
Ice, to fill blender

Mix limeade & vodka. Fill remainder of 5-cup blender container with ice. Pulverize. Serve frozen with mint sprigs.

Welu's Special Manhattan Cocktail

1 ounce grenadine
4 ounces Southern Comfort
4 ounces straight bourbon, no blends

8 ounces Martini & Rossi Sweet Vermouth

Add all ingredients. This will make 1 pint. If you double the recipe you can make a quart.

Pat's Eggnog

24	eggs, separated	1	quart heavy cream
2	cups granulated sugar	2	quarts milk
1	quart bourbon	1	quart vanilla ice cream
2	cups brandy		

Beat eggs yolks & sugar until thick. Add bourbon & brandy & stir thoroughly. The liquor "cooks" the eggs. Add cream & milk & continue whipping. Break up the ice cream & add. Beat egg whites until stiff & fold in. Refrigerate 30 minutes before serving. Sprinkle lightly with nutmeg. Serves 30.

Note: This is fairly potent so you might want to cut back the bourbon & brandy.

Laurie's Bloody Marys

1	fifth vodka	½	bottle lemon juice or fresh
1	46-ounce can tomato juice		lime juice
1	46-ounce can V-8 juice	1½	tablespoon salt
1	small bottle Lea & Perrins		pepper to taste
½	bottle Pick-A-Peppa		Tabasco to taste

Mix all ingredients. Serve with a celery stick in each glass, if desired. Drink heartily for this does not keep well. *Laurie makes these on Christmas morning and distributes them to needy parents.*

Margie's Favorite Christmas Wassail

1	cup sugar	1	cup water
12	whole cloves	2	2" cinnamon sticks
1	quart orange juice	3	quarts cranberry juice

Combine sugar, water and spices in large sauce pan. Simmer 10 minutes. Remove cloves. Add juices and heat.

Jane's Creamy, Smooth, Rich, Hot Chocolate

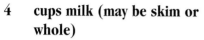

4	cups milk (may be skim or whole)	¼	cup cocoa powder
1	can sweetened condensed milk (may use reduced fat)	1	teaspoon cinnamon
		1	teaspoon nutmeg
		½	teaspoon vanilla

Combine all ingredients and simmer on low until heated and mixed thoroughly, stirring frequently. May top with whipped cream and sprinkle with chocolate sprinkles, if desired.

Angie's Hot Chocolate Mix

1	pound box powdered sugar	1	8-10 quart box powdered milk
1	2-pound box Nestle Quik	1	pound jar coffee creamer

Mix all ingredients together and blend well.

Note: To make 1 cup–Fill ⅔ of the cup with Hot Chocolate Mix and add boiling water to fill the remaining ⅓.

Brandy Freeze

½	gallon vanilla ice cream	¼	cup Kahlua
½-1	cup brandy, depending on how strong you like it		

Place all ingredients in blender and mix. Serve in champagne glasses. Servings 10-12.

Variation: Add a little instant coffee to taste.

Carol's Tea Punch

2	family sized tea bags	1	42 ounce can pineapple juice
1½	cups granulated sugar (or more to taste)	2	quarts water, boiling
			Sprigs of mint
1	6 ounce can frozen limeade		

While tea is steeping 5 minutes in 2 quarts hot water, add sprigs of mint. In gallon container add tea and sugar. When tea mixture is room temperature add limeade and pineapple juice. Pour over block of ice in punch bowl.

Thomas' Cinco Smoothies

| 2 | cups strawberries, fresh | Choice of other fruits |
| 1 | tablespoon sugar | |

In a blender, combine berries & sugar. It can be used as is, or you can add 1 cup of banana, peaches or other berries. You may add a cup of ice to make it a slush.

Note: Add 6 ounces of yogurt, milk, or ice cream to make it extra thick and yummy. Makes a healthy after school snack.

Elise's Jello Shots

| 1 | 6-ounce box Jello, any flavor | 2 | cups water, boiling |
| 2 | cups Vodka Citron | | |

Stir boiling water into Jello until it dissolves. Stir in 2 cups vodka. Pour into small shot glasses, cups or dixie cups. Refrigerate until firm. ***Cheers! Salud! Skol!***

CitaRita's

2	1.75-liter bottles of Jose Cuervo tequila, 1 gold & 1 clear	4	12-ounce cans frozen lemonade, thawed
1	liter bottle Triple Sec	4	quarts water
1	cup fresh squeezed lime juice, about 12 limes		

Combine all ingredients. Mix well. Place in large container (or several smaller ones) and freeze. Stir a few times during first day of freezing. These will keep indefinitely in freezer. To serve, remove about one hour beforehand and let get to slushy frozen Margarita consistency. Or, you can spoon out individual glasses as needed. Because of alcohol, this mixture will never get ice hard. May add more water if too strong. Serves a crowd.

Margaritas a la César

1	cup Jose Cuervo Gold Tequila	Ice
¼	cup Cointreau	Salt
¼	cup fresh squeezed lime juice	Limes, sliced

Place tequila, Cointreau, lime juice and some ice in a jug with a cover. Shake for about 3 minutes. Pour mixture (less the ice used) into Margarita glasses over fresh ice. Garnish with a slice of lime. Serves 5 people.

Note: For salt-rimmed glasses, pour a large amount of salt on a plate, wet the rim of the glass and dip glass into the salt.

Muppet

Fill a shot glass ¾ full of tequila. Top off with 7-Up. Cover & bang glass on table to fizz. Drink straight down. Instant joy!

Sugar Bustin' Tea

10	tea bags	1½	tablespoons vanilla extract
2	cups boiling water	1½	tablespoons almond extract
2	cups sugar		Fresh mint leaves
3	quarts water		Fresh lime, lemon,
1	6-ounce can frozen lemonade		pineapple, orange, sliced
1	6-ounce can frozen limeade		

Bring water to a boil & pour over tea bags. Cover & let steep 10-15 minutes (don't let it get bitter). Mix sugar & 3 quarts of water. Boil until sugar dissolves. Combine sugar water, tea, concentrates & flavorings & refrigerate. This is better after it sits for 8-12 hours. Serve over ice, garnished with fruit slices & mint. Very, very sweet, but delicious.

Frozen Cranberry Spritzer

1	32-ounce bottle Cranberry Juice Cocktail	1	28-ounce bottle ginger ale
		1½	cups bourbon, gin or vodka
1	12-ounce can frozen lemonade		

Thaw lemonade. Mix all ingredients. Freeze. Keep this in freezer for a refreshing summer cocktail.

Green Punch

1	6-ounce can lemon juice, frozen	6	6-ounce cans water
		1	quart rum
2	6-ounce cans limeade, frozen	1	quart ginger ale
1	6-ounce can orange juice, frozen		Green food coloring, or other choice of food coloring

Thaw and mix all ingredients. Add coloring to desired shade. Put in freezer. Serve slushy.

Note: Good choice for St. Patrick's Day or Derby Day.

Soups, Stews & Gumbos

Soups, Stews & Gumbos

Preceding Page: The Bruce Family
Top, left to right: Walter and Kay Bruce, Jerry Mischon, & Laurie; Kirk, Susan & Elizabeth Bruce.
Middle, left to right: Gib, Nicholas, and Emily Chapman.
Bottom: Cy, Walt Jr. & Thomas Bruce.

Almeta's Goose Gumbo

Almeta Scott cooked for many Houston families. We feel fortunate that she shared with us some of her famous recipes, of which gumbo is #1.

	Bacon grease or other grease	1	cup chopped onion
2	tablespoons flour	¼	cup chopped bell pepper
1	pound okra		Salt & pepper to taste
1	large can tomatoes	1	teaspoon gumbo file
1	tomato can of water	1	goose, cooked and cut up*
1	cup chopped celery		Tabasco, to taste

*Goose should be parboiled with onions, celery, apples and parsley for 20 minutes, refrigerated overnight, washed and roasted for 2½ hours at 325°. Or you may just reduce the heat after parboiling and cook until tender adding chicken broth or water. Add 2 tablespoons flour to grease in a large pot. Brown this very well. Add onions, celery, and bell pepper. Stir while cooking a few minutes. Add tomatoes, water, okra, salt & pepper. Cook slowly one hour or until vegetables are well done. Add goose plus gumbo file. I often add a few shakes of Tabasco. Serve over rice. Serves 8.

Variation: Substitute duck or shrimp & crab for goose.

Cathy C's Vegetable Soup

1	pound ground beef	1	can undiluted cream of
1	large chopped onion		mushroom soup
1	28-ounce can V-8 juice	2	packages frozen mixed
1	can undiluted cream of		vegetables
	celery soup	1	package frozen okra
			Salt & pepper, to taste

Brown meat and onion in an ungreased heavy pan. Add V-8 juice; gradually stir in soups. Bring to boil. Add vegetables and cook slowly until green beans are done. Serves 8.

Note: to lower the fat content, substitute ground turkey for the ground beef.

Gib's Granny D's Beef Stew

2	pounds beef stew meat	1	slice bread, crumbled
2-3	carrots, cut in large chunks	1	16-ounce can stewed tomatoes
1	onion, sliced	½	cup red wine
3	tablespoons Minute Tapioca		Salt & pepper, to taste

Put all ingredients in a casserole. Cook at 300° for 4 hours, stirring once.

Tomato Soup Treat

Tomato soup, your favorite
canned or packaged variety
Cottage cheese

Durkee's Canned French
Fried Onion Rings

In each mug of hot soup add 2-3 tablespoons cottage cheese & top with onions.

Cheese Potato Soup

1	10½-ounce can Campbell's Cream of Potato Soup	2	cans milk
1	10½-ounce can Campbell's Cheddar Cheese Soup	1	cup Cheddar cheese, grated
			Dash Tabasco

Combine all ingredients in saucepan. Heat to a slow boil, stirring occasionally. Add cheese & reduce heat until it has thoroughly melted. Serve hot.

Note: You can substitute Velveeta Cheese with the same delicious results.

Cream of Crab Soup

1 quart milk, cream or
Half & Half

2 tablespoons butter

1 tablespoon flour

1½ pound crabmeat

2 eggs, hard-boiled

1 lemon, grated peel only

1 teaspoon Worcestershire

½ cup sherry

Salt & pepper, to taste

Blend butter & flour in a double boiler. Add eggs which have been mashed, lemon peel & milk or cream. Stir until it thickens. Add the crabmeat. Let simmer 5 minutes. Add seasonings. Stir in sherry & heat thoroughly. Serves 6-8.

Hearty Taco Soup

1 pound lean ground turkey or
beef

1 packet taco seasoning mix

1 14½-ounce can beef broth

1 14½-ounce Italian style
tomatoes

1½ tomato cans of water

1 15-ounce can Ranch Style
Beans with jalapeños,
undrained

1 8-ounce can whole-kernel
corn, undrained

2 small carrots, peeled & diced

1 medium onion, chopped

2 garlic cloves, chopped

1 teaspoon chili powder

¼ teaspoon cayenne papper

½ teaspoon ground oregano

Salt, to taste

Dash Worcestershire

⅓ cup small pasta shells,
uncooked

Cheddar or Monterrey Jack
cheese, grated for topping

In a large pot, brown meat, adding a slight amount of oil to turkey if needed. Drain fat. Add seasoning mix, broth, tomatoes, water, beans, corn, carrots, onion, garlic, chili powder, cayenne, oregano, salt & Worcestershire & bring to a boil. Simmer 5 minutes. Add pasta & continue to simmer until pasta is tender, about 15 minutes. Turn off heat & let stand 5 minutes. Add more water to broth to adjust consistency, if desired. Garnish with cheese. Makes 4-6 servings.

Vichyssoise

1	chicken bouillon cube	1	cup ice, crushed
1	cup water, boiling	½	cup milk
½	small onion	½	cup heavy cream
½	teaspoon salt	4	chives (or green onion tops),
	Dash of pepper		chopped
1	16-ounce can potatoes, diced		

Dissolve chicken bouillon cube in the boiling water. Cool. Put in blender container and add onion, salt, pepper & potatoes. Blend on high about 10 seconds. Add crushed ice, milk & cream. Blend at high speed 10 seconds longer. Serve top with chives. Serves 4.

Catherine's Great Gumbo

1	stalk celery, chopped	1	20-ounce can tomatoes, crushed
1	large onion, chopped		
6	cloves garlic, minced	1	4-ounce can tomato sauce
1	tablespoon Creole Seasoning	2	pounds crabmeat
1	bag Zatarain's Crab Boil	2	pounds shrimp
1	cup of flour	1	pound crab claws
1	16-ounce package okra, frozen	6	cups water or chicken broth
			Salt & pepper, to taste

In a large cast iron skillet, brown the flour without adding oil. Stir constantly. Add broth, tomatoes & tomato sauce to flour, stirring in slowly so lumps don't form. Add vegetables and seasonings & cook until tender. Add crab boil bag which is spicy, so time according to your taste and remove. Add shrimp & cook until done (about 10 minutes). Add crab meat & claws and cook another 5 minutes, or until hot. Serve over rice.

Note: Of course you can add cooked chicken, sausage, oysters or fish according to your taste.

Harry's Crab Soup

1	quart buttermilk
1	cup fresh crab meat, large lumps
1	teaspoon salt
1	level teaspoon sugar, very important
1	cup cucumbers, peeled, seeded & diced
1	tablespoon dry mustard
1½	tablespoons fresh dill, or 2 teaspoons dry dill

Mix all ingredients together & chill as long as possible before serving. Serve with a thin, unpeeled slice of cucumber floating on top with a sprinkling of paprika. Serves 5 to 6.

Gazpacho Blanco

3	cucumbers
3	cups chicken broth
1	clove garlic
	Dash green Tabasco
3	tablespoons white wine vinegar
1	teaspoon salt
2	cups sour cream
	Dash pepper

Peel cucumbers deeply to remove any bitterness. Mix cucumbers, broth and garlic in blender or Cuisinart. Add remaining ingredients. Refrigerate 24 hours before serving. Serve with bowls of chopped tomato, avocado, celery, green onion, cilantro, almonds or pine nuts.

TR's Poblano Soup

3	tablespoons butter or oil	4	Poblano peppers, washed
1	onion, chopped	1	clove garlic, minced
2	tablespoons flour		Salt & pepper, to taste
3	10½-ounce cans chicken broth		

Broil chiles until skins are blistered (4-6 minutes). Turn until all sides are blistered. Transfer to brown paper bag until cool enough to handle. Peel off skin, seed & cut off stem. Chop chiles. Sauté onion in butter. Add flour & a little broth. Stir to make smooth roux. Add peppers & remaining broth. Serve hot.

Note: Soup can be put in a blender & a little cream or sour cream added for a thick soup. Spicy & good!

Bambe's Oyster Stew

1	gallon oysters	1	teaspoon Worcestershire
1	pound butter	1	teaspoon Tabasco
4	teaspoons salt	1	gallon milk
1	teaspoon celery salt	1	quart cream (regular)
1	teaspoon paprika		

Heat together in a pot, the first seven ingredients until the edges of the oysters curl. Heat 1 gallon milk & 1 quart cream in another pot until boiling point. Mix together.

Willie's Stew

2	pounds lean stew meat	1	bay leaf
	Shortening	2½	cups water
1	clove garlic	1	potato, diced
	Salt, to taste	1	16-ounce package frozen mixed
	Cracked fresh pepper, to taste		vegetables
1	large onion, chunks		Thin paste of flour & water
1	10¾-ounce can whole tomatoes		

Season stew meat with salt & pepper. Cover bottom of large pot with shortening and brown garlic clove. (Put toothpick in clove). Take garlic clove out and brown meat in garlic shortening. Add onion, can of tomatoes, bay leaf, & water. Cook covered for about 3 hours. Ten minutes before serving, add frozen mixed vegetable & potato. Add thickening last (flour & water mixed together to make a thin paste.)

Note: This makes a great meal served with rolls & salad.

Jane's Ultimate Baked Potato Soup

4	large baking potatoes	4	green onions, chopped
⅔	cup butter	12	slices bacon, cooked, crumbled
⅔	cup flour		& divided
6	cups milk	1¼	5-ounce package Cheddar
¾	teaspoon salt		cheese, shredded
½	teaspoon pepper	8	ounces sour cream

Boil potatoes, cut in cubes. Melt butter in a heavy saucepan over low heat; add flour, stirring until smooth. Cook one minute, stirring constantly. Gradually add milk, cook over medium heat, stirring constantly, until mixture is thickened & bubbly. Add potato pulp, salt, pepper, 2 tablespoons green onion, ½ cup bacon, & 1 cup cheese. Cook until thoroughly heated, stir in sour cream. Add extra milk if necessary for desired thickness. Top with remaining onion, bacon & cheese.

Spicy, Chicken-Rice Soup

1	chicken, cooked & deboned	1	teaspoon cumin
	or	3	cups of water with or without
4-8	chicken breast, boiled & cut up		chicken bouillon cubes
2	10½-ounce cans chicken broth	⅔	cup uncooked rice
3	10-ounce cans Rotel Tomatoes	1	16-ounce package frozen
	with Green Chilies, mild or spicy		yellow corn
1	14-ounce can tomatoes, chopped	½	cup fresh cilantro leaves, chopped
1	large onion, chopped	2	cloves garlic, chopped

Add to the chicken all remaining ingredients. Simmer long enough to heat thoroughly and cook rice.

Note: To serve, ladle soup in bowl. Garnish with grated cheddar cheese, or grated Monterey Jack cheese, chopped cilantro, chopped jalapeños, cubed avocados. Top with crumbled tortilla chips.

Crab Bisque

1	pound crab meat, lump or pieces	¾	tablespoon Worcestershire
1	can tomato soup	¼	teaspoon Tabasco
1	can green pea soup	5	tablespoons sherry
1½	pint Half & Half		Salt & pepper, to taste
¾	cup chicken broth		

Blend the soups & add liquid slowly. Place in double boiler. Add seasonings & sherry while stirring. Add crab meat 10 minutes before serving.

Note: This soup make a quick Sunday supper with hot muffins and a tossed green salad. We use this soup for entertaining, too. Serve from a soup tureen in small demitassé cups. It gives some substance to a buffet cocktail party. When doubling or making any large amount increase your liquid substantially and approximate your crab, then season to taste.

Wrightsville Beach Garden Soup

1	tablespoon olive oil	5	tablespoons ketchup
1	large bunch green onions	2	tablespoons Lawry Salt
2	large garlic cloves, peeled	2	tablespoons mixed pepper
2	sprigs thyme		kernels
3	sprigs dill *or* 1 tablespoon dried dill	2	tablespoons butter
5	cups fresh tomatoes, ripe & cut into 2" chunks	1½	cups water

In a large skillet, heat olive oil and add onions, garlic, thyme and dill for about 5 minutes. Then stir in ketchup, tomatoes, salt, pepper and 1½ cups of water. Bring to a boil. Cover and reduce to low and simmer for 15 minutes. Remove herb sprigs and any loose peel, add in butter and puree in blender. Top with Basil Oil when serving.

Basil Oil Dressing

4	cups basil leaves, loosely packed	2½	cups oil (Mazola or virgin olive oil)
1	teaspoon salt	6	cups water

Bring 6 cups of water to boil stirring in basil until bright green (30-45 seconds). Remove basil and press dry with paper towels. Mix ½ cup of oil with basil and salt and blend in mixer. Add remaining oil for 5 seconds. Use this mixture to make a small circle or design of choice on top of soup. Oil mixture will float on top if soup is already placed in cups or small bowls.

Matthew's Spicy Tomato Soup

2	10-ounce cans tomato soup	4	stems cilantro
2	10-ounce cans chicken broth	2	dashes cayenne pepper

Mix all ingredients & simmer 5 minutes. Remove cilantro & serve. Serves 4.

Note: This is also good poured over angel hair pasta.

Aunt Alice's Best Spinach Soup

1	package frozen spinach, chopped	2	tablespoons chicken stock
3	tablespoons butter, melted	1	cup boiling water
2	teaspoons red onion, chopped	2	cups milk
			or
1	teaspoon lemon juice	1	cup milk & 1 cup cream
			Salt & pepper, to taste

Cook spinach in lightly salted water. Drain thoroughly. Place spinach in a blender or food processor. Add butter, onion, lemon juice, chicken stock and water. Blend. Add milk and/or cream, salt & pepper. Blend very thoroughly & serve. Can be heated again or served cold.

Salads & Dressings

Salads & Dressings

Preceding Page: The Fauntleroy, Grainger and Cox Families

Top row, left to right: Robby, Glenda, Mitch, Matthew, John and Parker;

Bottom row, left to right: Parker, Ginny, Shelley, Mitchell, Fran, Lara and Rob.

Romaine Citrus Salad with Almonds

¼	cup vegetable oil		3	tablespoons granulated sugar
2	tablespoons vinegar		1	head romaine lettuce, torn
2	teaspoons granulated sugar		1	cup celery, chopped
1½	teaspoons fresh parsley, chopped		2	green onions, chopped
			1	avocado, chopped
½	teaspoons salt		1¼	cups mandarin oranges, drained
	Dash Tabasco			
⅓	cup almonds, slivered			

Combine oil, vinegar, 2 teaspoons sugar, parsley, salt & Tabasco in a bowl. Whisk until thoroughly mixed. Cover & chill in refrigerator. Combine almonds & 3 tablespoons sugar in a skillet & mix well. Cook over medium heat until nuts are coated and lightly brown. Stir constantly. Let stand until cool. Combine romaine, celery & onions in bowl & toss well. Add the almonds and avocado, tossing to mix. And last add the oranges.

Note: Pecans can be substituted for almonds for an equally great dish.

Apple, Pear, Goat Cheese Salad

	Select 3 types of lettuce (large handful per person)		1	stick goat cheese
			2	handfuls walnuts
1	pear, peeled			Oil & vinegar dressing
1	green apple, peeled			

Wash, dry & tear lettuce. Chill & crisp. A half hour before dinner, peel & slice the pear & apple. Shred goat cheese. Mix lettuce, apple, pear, goat cheese & walnuts in bowl. Toss with oil & vinegar dressing.

Korean Salad

½	head romaine lettuce		1	tablespoon Balsamic Vinegar
1	cucumber		½	clove garlic, crushed
½	red bell pepper		½	teaspoon salt
Dressing:				Pepper, to taste
¼	cup olive oil, extra virgin			Pinch of sugar

This is my favorite salad, I like it because it is a close substitute to kimchee, Korean pickled cabbage side dish which accompanies every Korean meal. Everyone has their own peculiar way with salads. I like to peel the cucumber, cut it in half lengthwise and take the seeds out and then cut into slices. I also like to cut the red bell pepper into thin julienned strips. The dressing needs to be mixed well before it is mixed with the salad.

Note: For variation, add feta cheese & olives. Top with walnuts.

Southwest Chicken Salad

1	cup cherry tomato halves		*Vinegarette Dressing:*	
1	cup corn, unfrozen		6	tablespoons olive oil, extra virgin
1	cup black beans, rinsed & drained		4	tablespoons red wine vinegar
½	cup cilantro, fresh chopped		1	teaspoon Dijon Mustard
½	cup red onion, finely chopped			Salt & ground pepper to taste
4	chicken breasts, cooked, skinless & sliced Romaine lettuce			

Dressing: Combine all ingredients in a small jar with a tight fitting lid. Shake well.

Salad: Mix together corn, beans, tomatoes, cilantro & red onions with 4 tablespoons of vinegarette. Then gently toss chicken into mixture and serve on romaine lettuce leaves.

Randy's Salad

2   Cooked chicken breasts, sliced & skinless (heat slightly)

1   package American salad greens, prewashed

2   green onions, chopped

2   green apples, peeled and chopped

1   8-ounce Bleu cheese, crumbled (optional)

Dressing:
Strawberry Dressing (at your local grocery store)

Combine lettuce, green onions, apple and bleu chesse together. Toss with Strawberry Dressing. Lay chicken slices on top of lettuce mixture.

Note: The wife can't mess this one up!

Bobby's Caesar Salad

1   egg yolk

4   anchovy filets, more if desired for garnish

¼   cup vinegar, Balsamic

4   cloves garlic, minced

1   teaspoon Worcestershire

1   tablespoon Dijon mustard

1   cup or more romano cheese, freshly shredded

    Salt and pepper, to taste

1   cup extra virgin olive oil

1   cup homemade croutons, optional

2½   heads romaine lettuce

Rub the inside of a large wooden bowl with a garlic clove half, then mix egg yolk with anchovies, vinegar, garlic, Worcestershire, mustard, salt and pepper and romano cheese, making a paste. Slowly whisk in oil. Mix or whisk until smooth. Add lettuce and toss until all leaves are coated. Top with croutons and reserve romano. Serves 6.

Lisa's Party Salad

1 head romaine lettuce
1 head red leaf lettuce
1 large avocado, sliced or chopped
1 bunch green onions, chopped
3 roma tomatoes, sliced
1 green pepper, chopped
   Croutons, Italian garlic
1 bottle La Martineque Blue Cheese Vinagrette salad dressing

Break lettuce into desired size pieces. Add rest of ingredients and toss. Serves 10.

Margaret's Pineapple Cranberry Salad

1½ cups crushed pineapple
1 package lemon Jello
2 tablespoons lemon juice
1 tablespoon grated orange peel
2 cups whole cranberry sauce, canned
½ cup pecans, finely chopped

Drain pineapple. Save juice and add enough water to make 1½ cups liquid. Heat and pour over Jello. Add pineapple and cranberry sauce. Mix. Add orange peel, lemon juice, and nuts. Place in mold and chill. Slice and serve on lettuce leaves and top with softened cream cheese.

Susan's Watergate Salad

1 large can crushed pineapple
1 cup chopped pecans
1 cup miniature marshmallows
1 package instant pistachio pudding mix
1 9-ounce container Cool Whip

Mix all ingredients together in a large bowl & chill.

Mimi's Molded Tuna Salad

1	package unflavored gelatin	¾	cup mayonnaise
¾	cup water or use water drained from tuna in can plus 2 ounces water	1	cup celery, chopped fine
		½	cup bell pepper, chopped fine
½	teaspoon salt	1	2-ounce jar diced pimentos
2	tablespoons lemon juice	1	can white tuna, drained & flaked
¼	teaspoon Tabasco		

Sprinkle gelatin in water to soften. Heat, stirring constantly until dissolved. Add salt, lemon juice, and tabasco. Cool in refrigerator. Mix all other ingredients into gelatin mixture and refrigerate again until jelled. Then add mayonnaise. Pour into loaf pan or mold of choice. Cover with plastic wrap and chill. When chilled firmly, unmold by placing a warm cloth on bottom of mold until mixture slightly unmolds; then turn onto plate and garnish with colorful vegetables or fruit. Serves 8-12.

Ann McCarroll's Strawberry Spinach Salad

In food processor, chop:
- 1   shallot finely

Add:
- ½   pint strawberries
- 3   tablespoons sugar
- ⅓   cup apple cider vinegar

Blend well and slowly add:
- 1   cup vegetable oil

Mix with:
- 20   ounces baby spinach
- 1   pint sliced strawberries
- 1   cup spicy walnuts
- 1   cup Feta cheese

Serve immediately.

Elizabeth's Primavera Salad

1	pound broccoli	1	pint cherry tomatoes, halved
1	12-ounce package bowtie pasta, uncooked	½	cup chopped fresh basil
1	10-ounce package fresh spinach	¼	cup chopped fresh parsley
		⅓	cup pine nuts, toasted
1	pound smoked turkey breast, cut into thin strips		Versatile vinaigrette

Remove broccoli leaves and cut off ends of stalks; cut into 1" pieces. Cook in boiling water for one minute; drain and plunge into cold water. Drain and chill.

Cook pasta according to package directions. Drain; rinse with cold water and drain again. Combine pasta and versatile vinaigrette, tossing to coat. Place in a large heavy-duty, zip-loc bag. Chill 2 hours or overnight. Remove stems from spinach; wash and pat dry. Combine spinach, broccoli, pasta, turkey and remaining ingredients, tossing gently. Yield: 8-10 servings.

Versatile Vinagrette

⅔	cup olive oil	1½	teaspoon salt
¼	cup white wine vinegar	1	tablespoon pepper
¼	cup water	1	clove garlic, pressed

Combine all ingredients in a jar. Cover jar tightly, and shake vigorously. Yield 1 cup.

Emily's Country Salad

	Bibb lettuce	Walnut halves
	Radicchio lettuce	Raspberry/walnut vinaigrette
1	small can mandarin oranges	dressing (Silver Palate or
	Gorgonzola cheese, crumbled	Ken's are good choices)

Toss all ingredients and serve immediately.

Kay's Cabbage Slaw

8	cups shredded cabbage	
2	cups seedless grapes	
1	cup toasted almonds	

Dressing:
- ¾ cup mayonnaise
- 2 tablespoons vinegar
- 1 teaspoon sugar
- 2 teaspoons prepared mustard
- 1 teaspoon salt

Toss cabbage, grapes and toasted almonds with dressing that has already been mixed. Serves 8.

Ellen Rutherford's Top Ramen Salad

½ red cabbage
½ green cabbage
1 bunch green onions
1 large green pepper
1 package sunflower seeds
1 package almonds, toasted
1 package sesame seeds, toasted

3 packages beef Top Ramen Noodles, set aside flavor packet

Dressing:
6 tablespoons vinegar
2 tablespoons sugar
1 cup salad oil
2 packages Top Ramen Seasoning

Mix together cabbages, onion & green pepper. At the last minute add seeds & almonds & toss with dressing.

Note: Shrimp & chicken may be added to make a complete entree.

Kirk's Mexican Salad

2	packages or heads romaine lettuce torn up	2	avocados
1	can Trappey's Jalapinto Beans, drained	1	box cocktail tomatoes, halved
		1	cup shredded low-fat cheddar cheese

Toss all ingredients with Vinagrette Dressing or Almeta's Dressing which is below is also delicious. Or you can use your favorite bottled variety. Serves 8-10.

Note: Add chunks of cooked chicken for a main meal treat.

Almeta's French Dressing

1	cup lemon juice	1	teaspoon pepper
1	teaspoon salt	3-4	pod of garlic
1½	cup olive oil		

Combine all ingredients.

Kay's Tuna & Spinach Salad

Spinach, washed & torn in bite-sized pieces	Goat cheese, crumbled (optional)
Avocado	Tuna (fresh or solid packed in water)
Cocktail tomatoes	
Green onions, chopped	
Pine nuts, toasted	Vinagrette Dressing

Toast nuts under broiler, stirring often. Combine remaining ingredients with vinagrette dressing (see page 42 or Almeta's Dressing above).

Maggie's Chicken Cilantro Salad

2	whole chicken breasts, grilled & chopped	3	green onions, finely chopped
½	cup celery, finely chopped	3	tablespoons Hellman's Mayonnaise
½	cup cilantro, finely chopped Juice of 2 lemons	½	teaspoon seasoned pepper or lemon pepper

Mix all ingredients well & chill.

Note: This recipe is just as delicious with canned tuna. Substitute chicken breasts with 1 12-ounce can solid white tuna in water. Drain & flake tuna prior to adding other ingredients.

Pea Salad

2	10-ounce packages frozen peas, thawed	2	cups green onions, chopped
10	slices bacon, broiled & crumbled	½	cup smoked, salted almonds
1	cup celery, finely chopped	½	pint sour cream, light

Mix all ingredients and chill.

Note: For a main dish luncheon salad, add chunks of cooked chicken and a sprinkle of dill!

Creamy Caesar Dressing

3	cloves fresh garlic, peeled	1	tablespoon lemon juice
¾	cup mayonnaise	1	teaspoon Worcestershire
1	2-ounce can anchovies, drained	1	teaspoon Dijon Mustard Salt & pepper, to taste
2	tablespoons fresh Parmesan cheese, grated		

Place all ingredients in a blender. Makes enough for 2 heads of Romaine lettuce or 10 people.

Mariquita's Chicken Salad

2   chicken breasts, cooked & chopped

1   cup cilantro, chopped

4   tablespoons olive oil

2   avocados, chopped

1   lime, squeezed

4   green onions, chopped

     Salt & pepper, to taste

Combine all ingredients and let stand for 10 minutes. Serve with tortilla chips. Doña Mariquita's chips are the best with this salad.

MariCuckoos Cilantro Mousse

1   cup cilantro leaves, packed

3   green onions, chopped

3   teaspoons Chicken Flavored Knorr Soup Mix

1   envelope Knox Gelatin

3   tablespoons water

1   cup lowfat sour cream

1   cup lowfat plain yogurt

Combine everything but the gelatin in blender until smooth. Soften gelatin in water & heat until dissolved. Add to other mixture & pour into a lightly oiled mold. Refrigerate until set.

Note: This may be served as hors d'oeuvres with crackers or served with a little mayonnaise or sour cream dressing on top.

Cucumber & Jícama Mexicana

1   jícama

1   cucumber

½   cup lime juice

     Dash red pepper

Wash & peel cucumbers deeply to eliminate bitterness. Do the same with the jicama and slice both into sticks or rounds. Place in flat bowl or platter. Squeeze lime juice over top & sprinkle lightly with cayenne.

Hearts of Palm & Artichoke Salad

2	14-ounce cans hearts of palm		2	cloves garlic, minced
1	15-ounce can artichoke hearts		2	tablespoons lemon juice, fresh
¾	cup canola oil		¾	teaspoon salt
¾	cup olive oil		½-¾	teaspoon black pepper
1	cup red wine vinegar		½	cup Parmesan cheese, fresh
	Dash Cayenne			& grated
1	head lettuce			

Drain hearts of palm & artichoke hearts & slice. Mix all ingredients except cheeses & lettuce. Marinate vegetables in dressing for 24 hours. At serving time, toss with cheese & lettuce, or serve in lettuce cup & sprinkle cheese on top.

Goodman Salad Oriental

1	small cabbage, shredded		¼	teaspoon seasoning salt
1	Chinese or Napa cabbage, shredded		3	tablespoons fresh lime juice
8	green onions, chopped		2	tablespoons water
½	cup cilantro, chopped		¼	teaspoon soy sauce
¼	cup mint, chopped		½	teaspoon Maggi Sauce
1	cup cooked chicken, shredded		2	tablespoons Wesson Stir Fry Oil
½-¾	cup peanuts, unsalted		½	teaspoon Asian oil
	Ginger, to taste		1	drop hot-chili oil
¼	teaspoon black pepper			

Combine all seasonings, oils, lime juice & water. Put 2 slices of fresh ginger into seasonings mixture. Let stand at least 2 hours. Thoroughly toss cabbages, onions, cilantro & mint. When ready to serve add dressing & top with peanuts. Top with shredded chicken.

John's Spinach Salad

2 bunches or 1 bag fresh spinach
6 green onions, chopped
1 cup cherry tomatoes, halved

5 slices bacon, cooked crisp & crumbled
1 4-ounce package cream cheese
1 cup Cheddar cheese, grated

Wash, drain & remove stems from spinach. Make tiny balls out of cream cheese. Combine spinach, onions, tomatoes, bacon & add cream cheese balls. Mix well & add grated cheese. Top with dressing recipe below.

Dressing:
¼ teaspoon salt
¼ teaspoon Lawry's Seasoning Salt
¼ teaspoon garlic salt
¼ teaspoon dry mustard
¼ teaspoon black pepper

6 tablespoons lemon juice
1 teaspoon red wine vinegar
2 tablespoons water
½ teaspoon Maggi Sauce (soy sauce)
½ cup olive oil, or half olive & canola

Mix ingredients well & pour over Spinach Salad. Keep leftover dressing refrigerated.

Cliffe's Coleslaw

1 head cabbage, shredded
1 pint sour cream
1 cup mayonnaise
½ cup white vinegar
1 teaspoon black pepper

1 teaspoon celery salt
1 teaspoon seasoning salt
½ onion, grated
1-3 tablespoons dill pickle juice

Place shredded cabbage in a plastic bag & keep very cold. Mix remaining ingredients & refrigerate until serving time. The dressing is better if it sits for 6-24 hours. Toss slaw with dressing just before serving. This is very tart & crispy.

Isla's Layered Salad

1	pound fresh spinach		1	onion, sliced thin
4	hard boiled eggs, sliced (optional)		8	green onions, chopped
1	pound bacon, cooked crisp & crumbled		1½	cups mayonnaise
1	small head iceberg lettuce, shredded		¾	cup sour cream
1	10-ounce package frozen English peas, thawed		1	tablespoon lemon juice
			½	teaspoon celery salt
				Seasoning salt & pepper, to taste
			3	cups Swiss cheese, shredded

Wash, pick and tear spinach. Drain well. In a very large bowl, layer spinach, salt & pepper, eggs, bacon, lettuce, more salt & pepper, onions & peas. Repeat layers. Mash down a little, cover & refrigerate overnight. Combine mayonnaise, sour cream, lemon juice, celery salt, green onions & refrigerate also. In the morning, spread dressing over salad, covering well, completely to the sides of the container. Top with cheese. Refrigerate until lunch or dinner–the longer the better. Slice and serve. This can be topped with pinenuts or avocado slices.

Note: The green onions may be spinkled over the top for garnish instead of in the dressing. Thinly sliced water chestnuts can also be added to the layers. For variety, Parmesan cheese can be used instead of Swiss cheese, and the dressing can be made with ½ package of dry original Ranch Buttermilk Dressing added to the mayonnaise mixture.

James' Caesar Salad Dressing

1-2	cloves garlic, minced		1	egg yolk
5	anchovies		2	tablespoons red wine vinegar
½	teaspoon dry English mustard Dash Worcestershire			Juice of ½ a lemon
4	ounces olive oil, extra virgin		3	tablespoons Parmesan cheese Black pepper, to taste

Mix all ingredients in a blender except Parmesan cheese and pepper. Chill. Add pepper & cheese when tossing salad.

Aunt Mary's Fruit Salad Dressing

1½	cups salad oil		1½	teaspoon salt
1	cup sugar		½	small onion, grated
⅛	cup celery salt		½	cup vinegar
1½	teaspoon dry mustard			

Mix celery seed, sugar, mustard, salt & vinegar. Grate onion into oil & gradually add to other mixture.

Mimi's Yum-Yum Salad

1	package lime jello		½	pint whipping cream, stiffly whipped
1	cup Velveeta cheese, grated			
1	cup pecans, chopped		1	large can crushed pineapple, drained & retained
1	cup sugar			
			1	cup boiling water

Soften jello in hot water. Add pineapple. Heat sugar & pineapple juice until sugar dissolves. Add cheese & cool. Blend in the remaining ingredients. Pour in mold of choice & refrigerate.

Bybo's Apple Salad Mold

1	package lemon flavored jello		⅔	cup cabbage, chopped
1	cup boiling water		¼	cup pimientos, chopped
1	tablespoon lemon juice		¼	cup olives, chopped
⅔	cup orange juice		⅛	teaspoon salt
1	cup diced apples			

Dissolve jello in hot water. Cool & add fruit juices. Chill until mixture thickens. Stir in remaining ingredients & pour into mold. Chill.

Scottie Stevenson's Easy Shrimp New Orleans

3	dozen medium to large cooked shrimp, shelled & deveined	1	clove garlic, minced
		½	cup French dressing
		¼	jar creamed horseradish
1	medium onion, chopped	2	tablespoons spicy mustard

Mix all ingredients together & refrigerate overnight. Can be served as a salad or a heavy appetizer.

Mimi Stewart's 3-Layer Pineapple Delight Salad

1st Layer:
- 2 packages lemon Jello
- 4 cups water, hot
- 1 drop green food coloring
- 1 No. 2 can crushed pineapple, drained

Mix Jello, hot water, food coloring. Refrigerate; when starting to jell add pineapple and mix. Pour in container or mold and refrigerate until jelled.

2nd Layer:
- ½ cup whipping cream or Dream Whip
- 1 large package cream cheese, softened

Beat together until spreadable; add on top of 1st layer.

3rd Layer:
- ¾ cup sugar
- 2 tablespoons flour
- 2 tablespoons lemon juice
- 2 eggs, beaten
- 1 cup pineapple juice, reserved from above

Cook all ingredients until thick. Cool completely & spread on 2nd layer. Refrigerate again & sprinkle with grated cheese (if desired) when ready to serve.

Gladys Harrison's Cranberry Chicken Salad

1	envelope gelatin, unflavored		*Topping:*
¼	cup cold water	1	large can jellied cranberry
½	cup milk		sauce
1	cup celery, chopped	1	envelope gelatin, unflavored
½	cups parsley, chopped	¼	cup cold water
1	cup mayonnaise	1	9-ounce can pineapple,
2	cups cut-up cooked chicken		crushed & juice
	breast	½	cup pecans, chopped
	Salt & pepper, to taste		

Dissolve 1 envelope gelatin in cold water. Heat milk & add gelatin. When cooled, add celery, parsley & mayonnaise. Mix & add chicken, salt & pepper. Pour into a greased dish & chill until firm. Add topping.

Topping: In a double boiler, put cranberry sauce. Melt over heat & add remaining gelatin & cold water into mixture. Mix well & top on chicken salad. Cool overnight.

Rice Salad

2	7-ounce boxes Uncle Ben's chicken flavored rice, cooked	⅓	cup light mayonnaise
4-6	green onions, chopped	½	teaspoon curry powder
2	6-ounce jars marinated artichoke hearts, do not drain	2	cups sliced cooked carrots

Chop onions and artichokes; slice carrots and combine with artichokes & marinade, mayonnaise and curry powder. Add cooked rice and toss with mayonnaise mixture. Refrigerate. Serves 10-12.

Fruits, Vegetables & Sauces

Fruits, Vegetables & Sauces

Preceding Page: The Glauser Family
Top row, left to right: Vince, Alicia, Gloria & William.
Bottom, left to right: Pat & Ronnie.

Kiki's Spanish Green Beans

2	strips bacon, raw & chopped	1½	cups canned tomatoes, drained
¼	cup onion, chopped	1½	cups green beans, drained
2	tablespoons green pepper, chopped	¼	of 10-ounce can Rotel tomatoes, drained

Sauté bacon, onion & peppers until brown. Combine with remaining ingredients and place in a casserole dish. Bake at 350° for 30 minutes.

Ellen's Green Beans & Bacon

2	cans cut green beans	1	onion, chopped
1	can beef stock soup		Salt & pepper, to taste
8-10	pieces raw pepper bacon, cut up		

Cook over medium heat for 1½ hours.

Willie's Cabbage & Field Peas

1	10-ounce package frozen field peas	2	tablespoons margarine or butter
1	small head cabbage, shredded		Cracked pepper, to taste
1	onion, sliced	1	cup water, salted
	Juice of 1 lemon		

Cook peas in salted water for 15 minutes. Place shredded cabbage on top of peas. Top peas with the onion slices. Add margarine & cook until peas & cabbage are crunchy (about 15 more minutes). Drizzle lemon juice over top and add cracked pepper.

Note: I like to add a dash of vinegar.

Folly Hill Onion Casserole

5	jumbo onions, sliced	2	sticks butter, melted
16-20	Ritz crackers	2	tablespoons milk
2	cups Parmesan cheese, grated		Salt & pepper, to taste

Peel & slice onions. Cook in salted water until done. Drain. Butter an 8" casserole dish. Layer ⅓ of each of the onions, salt, pepper, crackers, butter & cheese. Repeat 2 times more & finish with cheese on top. Sprinkle milk over top. Bake at 350° for 20-30 minutes.

Robby's Cuban Black Beans

1	pound dried black beans	4	14½-ounce cans chicken broth
1	cup carrots, chopped	1	tablespoon salt
1	cup onions, chopped	1	teaspoon cayenne papper
1	cup celery, chopped	¼	pound bacon, chopped
½	cup parsley, chopped	1	teaspoon black pepper
1	14½-ounce can tomatoes, chopped	5	cloves garlic, chopped

Sauté bacon & add all vegetables. Sauté vegetables until translucent. Add beans and remaining ingredients except garlic. Cover beans with 1" of liquid (chicken broth or water). Simmer until beans are tender, about 1½-2 hours. If you need more liquid add water. Add the garlic 10 minutes before serving & continue to simmer.

Note: Serve with rice & a touch of sherry.

Mary's Fresh Corn Casserole

10-12 ears white or yellow corn
1½ stick butter
1-2 bunches of green onions, finely chopped
¼ cup jalapeño pepper, finely chopped
Salt and pepper, to taste
1 cup buttered bread crumbs

Remove kernels from ears of corn and place in a buttered casserole. Use a 9x11" Pyrex casserole but other will work as well. Melt 1 stick butter in skillet, add jalapeño peppers, salt and pepper. Pour into corn and mix lightly with dots of remaining butter. Top with bread crumbs. Bake at 325-350° for 30-40 minutes. Serves 12-15.

Eileen's Corn Casserole

1 stick melted margarine
1 can cream style corn
1 can regular corn, undrained
1 package Jiffy corn bread mix
2 eggs beaten
Cheddar cheese, grated

Mix together. Place in 9x12" Pyrex dish. Sprinkle with cheddar cheese. Bake uncovered at 350°.

Kay's Tomato Casserole

Tomatoes, sliced
Sour cream
Parmesan cheese
Canned French Fried Onions
Salt & pepper, to taste

Alternate layers of tomatoes (which have been salted & peppered), sour cream, and parmesan cheese. Top with French fried onions and bake in 350° oven until bubbly, about 35 minutes.

Zucchini Casserole

¼	cup uncooked rice		Pepper
1	zucchini, quartered & sliced		Garlic salt, to taste
	Several tomatoes, sliced	2-3	cups Velveeta cheese, grated

Layer rice, & remainder of ingredients in casserole. Repeat layers except for rice. Bake 45 minutes at 350°.

Mother's Squash

3-4	pounds yellow squash		Dash salt
1	medium onion, minced	1	teaspoon seasoned salt
2	bay leaves		Dash Worcestershire
6	sprigs parsley	1⅓	cup Swiss cheese, grated
½	teaspoon thyme	3	eggs
6	tablespoons butter		Cayenne pepper
3	tablespoons all-purpose flour		Buttered bread crumbs
			Nutmeg

Cut squash in ⅓" slices. Place in a large saucepan with onion, bay leaves, parsley and thyme. Cover with well salted water and bring to a boil. Cook slowly until squash is barely tender. Drain. Remove parsley & bay leaves. Mash squash and add butter, seasoned salt, dash of nutmeg & Worcestershire. Sprinkle in flour. Add 3 beaten eggs. Stir in 1 cup of the cheese & cayenne pepper. Pour in a buttered casserole. Mix remaining cheese with buttered bread crumbs. Sprinkle on top. Bake at 350° for 35 minutes. Serves 10.

Mitchell's Spinach Stuffed Squash

1   10-ounce package frozen
    spinach in butter sauce,
    thawed & cooked
4   medium to large yellow
    squash

½   cup Mozarella cheese
4   strips bacon, fried & crumbled
    Few shakes Pic-a-Peppa
    Sauce

Cut squash in half and scoop out center. Steam squash about 5 mnutes in small amount of water in the microwave. Remove steamed squash & drain. Stuff squash with cooked spinach and place in Pyrex dish. Top with Mozzarella cheese, a dollop of Pic-a-Peppa, and cooked bacon if desired. Bake at 350° until cheese melts, about 15-20 minutes.

Nancy's Squash Casserole

3   pounds yellow squash,
    sliced
3   eggs
1   cup mayonnaise, light
2   small onions, chopped

1   cup grated Parmesan cheese,
    Kraft or fresh
10 Ritz Crackers
    Salt & pepper, to taste
    Butter

Cook squash & onion until just tender. Drain in colander. Mash water out. Beat eggs. Add mayonnaise and Parmesan cheese to eggs. Add all to squash. Pour into buttered baking dish. Dot the top of the squash mixture with butter. Top casserole with crumbled Ritz Crackers immediately before baking. Bake at 350° for 20-35 minutes until center is hot. If this is to be rewarmed place cracker crumbs on at the end.

Carmen's Green Beans

2	cans whole Blue Lake Green Beans	¼	cup water
½	cup ketchup	½	cup pear juice
¼	cup sweet pickle juice	½	cup pineapple juice
		5	slices bacon

Wrap 8 green beans with half a slice of bacon. Repeat until all the beans are wrapped. To make the sauce, combine ketchup, pickle juice, water, pear & pineapple juice. Place beans in a shallow casserole dish & cover with sauce. Bake uncovered at 400° for 30 minutes. Add water to keep beans from burning if sauce evaporates. Serves 6

Sautéed Tomatoes

3	large homegrown tomatoes, quartered	3	tablespoons basil, chopped (or 6 leaves)
½	cup olive oil		Seasoned salt, to taste
6	cloves of garlic, crushed or 1 tablespoon minced garlic		Pepper, to taste

Wash tomatoes and quarter. Five minutes before dinner is served. Heat oil and minced garlic in large skillet, add tomatoes. Cook quickly until slightly tender. Sprinkle with fresh basil. Season with seasoning salt & pepper. Cook 1 minute. Serve hot.

T's Fried Green Tomatoes

1	green tomato, sliced ¼-inch thick	½	teaspoon salt
¼	cup corn meal	½	teaspoon white pepper
¼	cup flour or corn flour	¼	cup olive oil, butter or bacon grease
¼	teaspoon sugar		

Mix dry ingredients. Dip tomatoes into mixture and cook in your choice of oil until just crisp. Makes a delightful sandwich with a little mayonnaise, bacon and fresh basil.

Note: My Daddy grows tomatoes so we pick and fry them. Firm red tomatoes will work almost as well.

Carrot Soufflé

5   medium carrots, about ½ pound

2   tablespoons onion, minced

4   tablespoons butter or margarine

3   tablespoons flour

½   teaspoon salt

¼   teaspoon nutmeg
    Red pepper, to taste

1   cup milk

3   eggs, separated
- egg yolks beaten separately
- egg whites, whipped

Wash, but do not scrape, carrots; cut into 1½ pieces. Cook, covered in boiling salted water until tender; drain & puree in an electric blender, making ¾ of a cup. Sauté onion in butter until limp but not brown; stir in flour and seasonings. Slowly add milk, stirring until thickened. Add pureed carrot & cool slightly. Add beaten egg yolks & cool to lukewarm; fold in beaten egg whites. Pour into an ungreased 1 quart casserole; bake at 350° for 35-40 minutes until center is firm. Serves 4-6.

Laurie's Marinated Vegetables

Cucumbers

Squash

Artichoke hearts

Hearts of palm

Carrots

Green beans (canned Blue Lake variety)

Green onions, chopped

Cook squash and carrots slightly. Cut lengthwise. Cut other vegetables (except chopped green onions) and cover all with dressing. I use Le Martinque French or Newman's Italian. Almeta's Dressing (page 44), is especially good. Chill well for 4 hours or longer. Serve over lettuce and sprinkle with chopped green onions.

Bambe's Chile Rellenos

3	4-ounce cans sliced green chili peppers, drained	1	pound Monterrey Jack cheese, grated
1	pound Cheddar cheese, grated	3½	cups milk
		½	cup flour
5	eggs	1	teaspoon salt

Dry the well drained peppers on paper toweling. Place on bottom of 9½x13" baking dish & cover with cheeses. Beat the eggs, add flour, milk & salt. Pour over the cheese. Bake at 350° for 50 minutes or until custard sets & top is golden brown. Serve from baking dish.

Note: When entertaining, make this ahead and reheat at 350° for 30 minutes. It won't rise quite as high, but the guests won't know the difference. Serves 8.

Kitty's Onion Tarte

1	9" pastry shell, baked	4	tablespoons flour
2	medium onions, coarsely chopped	¾	cup Swiss cheese, grated
2	tablespoons butter	2	tablespoons Parmesan cheese, grated
5	eggs		Dash of nutmeg
2½	cups milk		

Prebake pastry shell in 400° oven until lightly browned. Sauté onions in butter until translucent. Meanwhile, mix eggs & milk well. Add flour moistened with a little milk, and whisk until smooth. Cook mixture quickly in saucepan, stirring constantly. Add Swiss & Parmesan cheeses. Stir until smooth. Add salt, pepper, nutmeg & cooked onions. Pour into pastry shell & bake at 350° for 30 minutes, or until slightly browned.

Fruits, Vegetables & Sauces

Vince's Mustard Greens

4-6	bunches greens, any type		Salt & pepper, to taste
3-4	slices bacon, cut in quarters		Pinch seasoned salt
3½	cups water		Pinch Accent
1	jalapeño pepper	2	pinches granulated sugar

Pick & wash greens 5-6 times until clean. Cook bacon in pot until done. Add water & bring to a boil. Add greens & cook 25-30 minutes. Add seasonings, sugar & jalapeño pepper. Cook until greens are tender, approximately 30-45 minutes.

Note: You must taste to see if they are done. Made by Ola at least once a week.

Baked Beans

1	pound ground chuck	1	green pepper
2	16-ounce cans pork & beans	½	cup chili sauce
		1	teaspoon prepared mustard
1	medium onion, chopped	½	cup brown sugar
2	green onions, chopped	½	teaspoon garlic powder

Brown meat seasoned with salt & pepper. Drain well. Combine remainder of ingredients. Add meat & place in medium size casserole dish. Cover & bake at 400° for 30 minutes. *Ummmmm Good!*

Fresh Spinach

1½	ounces extra virgin olive oil	1	jalapeño pepper
1	teaspoon garlic, sliced		Salt & pepper, to taste
1	package spinach, fresh		

Sauté spinach in olive oil. Add remaining ingredients & cover. Simmer until tender. Serves 2, but can be doubled or tripled.

Fresh Spinach Casserole

1	package fresh spinach, washed & chopped	1	teaspoon salt
3	eggs, well beaten	2	cups creamed cottage cheese
6	tablespoons flour	2	cups Cheddar cheese, grated
			Pepper to taste

Beat eggs & flour until smooth. Mix the remaining ingredients. Bake uncovered in a 2 quart casserole dish for 1 hour at 350°. Let stand a few minutes before serving. Serves 8-10.

Garlic Broccoli

1	bunch broccoli	1½	tablespoons olive oil
2	teaspoons fresh lemon juice		Salt & pepper to taste
1	clove garlic, finely chopped		

Cut broccoli into florets. Steam covered 4-5 minutes until crunchy. Heat oil, lemon juice, salt, pepper, and garlic until bubbly. Toss broccoli with garlic mixture and serve.

Carrots in Chicken Broth

2	10½-ounce cans of chicken broth	4-6	carrots
			Pepper, to taste

Peel carrots & slice into medallions. Cook carrots in broth at medium-high temperature until tender, approximately 25 minutes.

Randa's Jalapeño Corn Casserole

12	ounces cream cheese	3-4	fresh jalapeños, seeded & chopped
½	cup milk	4	12-ounce cans white shoe-peg corn, drained
4	tablespoons milk		
½	teaspoon black pepper		
1	teaspoon garlic salt		

Preheat oven to 350°. In a saucepan, place cream cheese, milk, butter & garlic salt. Cook over low heat stirring until mixture is melted forming a sauce. Remove from heat. Mix in jalapeños and corn. Pour into a 9x12" glass baking dish & bake 30 minutes.

Carroll's Corn

3	15-ounce cans yellow corn	1	8-ounce package cream cheese
3	15-ounce cans white corn	1	medium onion, chopped
3	4-ounce cans green chilies, chopped	1	tablespoon butter
1	cup bread crumbs	¼	cup milk
½	cup Parmesan cheese, grated	1	egg

Drain corn & chilies & mix well. Sauté onion in butter until translucent. Add cream cheese to onions & stir until smooth. Add cream cheese & onions to corn & chilies mixture. Beat egg & milk & add to mixture. Pour into a glass baking dish and top with Parmesan cheese & bread crumb mixture. Bake at 350° for 40 minutes.

Gail's Tomato Pie

1	9" pie crust, deep dish	2	cups grated Cheddar cheese
5	sliced tomatoes	1	cup mayonnaise
1	bunch green onions, chopped	½	cup Parmesan cheese, grated
1	bunch fresh basil, chopped		Salt & pepper, to taste

Place sliced tomatoes on paper towel to drain. Pierce bottom of pie shell & bake at 400° for 10 minutes. Let pie crust cool. Mix cheddar cheese & mayonnaise & set aside. Layer tomatoes, green onions, basil, salt & pepper, and top with cheese & mayonnaise mixture. Repeat until all the ingredients are used. Sprinkle top with Parmesan cheese & bake at 325° for 45 minutes.

Nanoo's Cranberries

1	16-ounce can cranberry sauce, jellied	1	cup frozen strawberries, thawed & drained
1	8-ounce can crushed pineapple, drained	1	cup frozen raspberries, thawed & drained
1	teaspoon vanilla		

Mix cranberry with electric mixer. Add other fruits & vanilla. Cover & refrigerate. Put in Granny's favorite crystal bowl on Thanksgiving table.

Fruits, Vegetables & Sauces

Margaret Fraser's Fruit Pizza

Mix with dough cutter until crumbly:

¾ **cup butter**
⅓ **cup powdered sugar**
1½ **cups flour**

Spread on ungreased pizza pan. Press down to form big cookie. Bake at 300° for 20 minutes or until edges are light brown. Cool.

Filling:

8 **ounces soft cream cheese**
½ **cup sugar**
1 **teaspoon vanilla**

Spread on cooled cookie. Arrange on filling, fresh fruit on top, blueberries, strawberries, bananas, peaches, pineapple, & other seasonal berries.

Top with cool glaze:

2 **tablespoons cornstarch**
½ **cup sugar**
1 **cup pineapple juice**
1 **teaspoon lemon juice**

Heat to boiling & boil 1 minute. Cool & top fruit pizza.

Betsy's Blue Applesauce

6-8 **apples, tart**
1¼ **cups granulated sugar**
½ **teaspoon blue food coloring**
Juice of 1 lemon

1½ **cups apple juice**
1 **teaspoon cinnamon**

Peel, core & slice apples into chunks. Cook in apple juice about 15 minutes. Add sugar & cinnamon & mash. Add food coloring. Good hot or cold.

Mom's Fool Proof Hollandaise Sauce

3	egg yolks		Pinch of cayenne pepper
2	tablespoons lemon juice	½	cup butter, melted
¼	teaspoon salt		

Blend in blender, egg yolks, lemon juice, salt and cayenne pepper. In a microwave container, heat butter covered on high for 3 seconds. Remove lid and pour over the eggs in a steady stream while blending on low. This takes about 30 seconds. If the sauce is not smooth, blend on high for 5 seconds. Serve at once or keep warm. Makes 1 cup.

Blender Hollandaise

2	sticks butter	pinch	cayenne pepper
4	egg yolks	¼	teaspoon salt
2	tablespoons lemon juice		

In small saucepan heat butter just to bubbling. Meanwhile, put egg yolks, lemon juice, salt & cayenne into electric blender. Cover container and turn blender on high speed. Immediately remove cover & add hot butter in a steady stream. The secret is to add butter fast, do not let mixture get too hot or it will separate. To keep, store in refrigerator. I fix it about once every two weeks & have it to spruce up vegetables during the week. When you begin cooking dinner, take the hollandaise out of the refrigerator and put in position near the stove. Stir it once or twice in the container. It will be room temperature by dinner & warm enough to put on your vegetables.

Fish & Seafood

Fish & Seafood

Preceding Page: The Reckling, Roach, McConn, & Goodman Families
Top row, left to right: Luke, James, Margaret, Cliffe, Angie, John, Michelle, Thomas, Randa, Doug,
Stephen & John.
Bottom row, left to right: Christiana, Elise, T.R., Isla, Galen & Carroll.

Dear God, Thank you for the stars that fill the sky, The birds that fill the air, The fish that fill the
waters, The creatures that fill the Earth, Thank you for filling us.

Judy Lee's Hot Crabmeat Sandwich

1	stick butter	½	teaspoon garlic salt
1	jar old English cheese	1	7- ounce can crab meat
	spread	6	English muffins
½	tablespoon mayonnaise		

Mix first 5 ingredients. Use extra mayonnaise if necessary and spoon on English muffin. Bake at 400° until bubbly, cut into quarters. Serve warm.

Lisa's Fish Boats

6	pieces white fish (catfish,	1	jar pico de gallo
	trout, snapper, etc.)	1	lemon, juiced
½	stick butter		Salt and pepper, to taste

Preheat oven to 350°. Place each piece of fish on a piece of aluminum foil large enough to completely cover fish. Dot each piece with butter on top and bottom. Sprinkle with lemon juice. Place 2-3 tablespoons of pico de gallo on top. Add salt and pepper. Wrap fish and place in oven for 20 minutes. Serves 6.

Note: Substitutes for pico de gallo
   1. *Vegetables sliced thinly and placed on fish*
   2. *Sauces of choice*

Margaret's Cajun Remoulade Sauce

3	tablespoons cajun mustard	1	tablespoon parsley, chopped
1	cup mayonnaise		Juice of 1 lemon
3	tablespoons capers,		Cayenne pepper, to taste
	chopped		

Combine all and serve as a dipping sauce for shrimp, crab claws or other seafood.

Mimi's Hot Shrimp Toast

1	pound shrimp, raw and shelled	2	teaspoons salt
1	(5 ounce) can water chestnuts, drained	1	teaspoon sugar
		1	egg, beaten
¼	cup green onions, chopped	15	slices thin bread
			Fine bread crumbs

In food processor, blend shrimp, water chestnuts, and onions. Add salt, sugar and egg. Spread on bread slices. Sprinkle lightly with bread crumbs. Cut each slice in 4 triangles. Fry in hot oil, 1" deep, with shrimp side down, then other side, about 2 minutes on each side. Drain and serve.

Note: Can be frozen after prepared. First defrost and reheat in oven for 5 minutes.

Oysters Erminie

1	quart oysters, semi-defrosted	1	package Peppridge Farm Herb Dressing mix
6	green onions		Salt & pepper, to taste
1	white onion	1	clove garlic
4	stalks celery		Parsley
	Butter		

Chop oysters fine while semi-defrosted. Brown green onions, white onion, and celery in butter. Add most of the package of Pepperidge Farm Herb Dressing mix, plus a little water if necessary. Add salt, pepper & garlic. Place in shells & sprinkle chopped parsley on top. Bake in 350° oven for about 30 minutes. Serves 8.

Tom Kelly's Snapper

	Snapper or white fish filets	⅓	cup white wine
1	large onion	5-6	tablespoons soy sauce
1-2	tomatoes, sliced		Salt & pepper, to taste
⅔	jar pimento		Bread crumbs
	Fresh mushrooms, sliced		Tabasco, to taste

Place thinly sliced onions in bottom of casserole. Add pimento. Rub fish filets with Tabasco & place on top of onions & pimento. Cover with fresh mushrooms and sliced tomatoes. Add wine, soy sauce, salt & pepper. Top with bread crumbs & bake in 350° oven for 30 minutes.

Trout La Marye/Almondine

5	medium size trout fillets, deboned		Flour for dredging
			Salt & red pepper, to taste
	Milk	1	lemon
	stick butter for frying fish	½	cup Sautérne wine

Cover fillets with milk for 20-30 minutes. Heat butter in pan over medium heat, being careful not to burn it. Remove fish from milk. Salt & pepper & dredge each filet in flour. Fry until light brown in color. Do not over cook. Remove fish from pan & place on heated platter. Squeeze lemon & pour wine into pan. Let simmer for 3-4 minutes. Pour same over fish & serve immediately.

Note: Add more butter for frying if necessary.
Variation: Lightly brown 1¼-1½ cups sliced almonds, in ½ stick butter placed in heavy skillet. Add to wine and lemon and sauté for 3-4 minutes. Pour over fish and serve immediately. If desired, add chopped parsley.

Crabmeat Sharman

2	8-ounce packages cream cheese, softened	2	tablespoons milk
2	tablespoons mayonnaise	13	ounces crabmeat, fresh
4	tablespoons grated onion		Juice of 1 lemon
1	tablespoon cream-style horseradish		Lea & Perrins Worcestershire

Mix all ingredients together until smooth. Top with paprika. Bake in 10-ounce buttered pie plate for 30 minutes at 350°.

Note: Recipe makes a great main dish or hot dip. Serve with sesame or rye Old London Melba rounds and toast. Crabmeat Sharman and a good salad makes quite a meal. Serves 6 as a main course, or 20 as a dip.

Hot or Not Poblano Sauce

¾	cup corn	1	tablespoon garlic, minced
¾	cup corn tortillas, chopped	1	cup tomato, chopped & seeded
3	roasted, peeled, seeded or not poblanos, cut into strips	1½	cups chicken stock
1	tablespoon shallots, minced		Salt and pepper

Spray frying pan with non stick cooking spray. (I use olive oil). Sauté shallots and garlic. Add remaining ingredients and sauté. Serve on top of your favorite fish filet. Serves 4 to 6.

Tartar Sauce

1	quart mayonnaise	¼	cup Dijon Mustard
½	onion, chopped	1	bunch green onions, finely chopped
¼	cup capers, chopped	1	dill pickle, finely chopped
2-3	cloves garlic, minced	½	cup cilantro, chopped
¼	cup parsley, minced		Juice of 1 lemon
3	fresh jalapeño peppers, finely chopped		

Mix all ingredients & refrigerate.

Robby's Crawfish Etouffée

2	pounds frozen crawfish tails, thawed	2	sticks butter
1½	cups onion, chopped	½	cup flour
1½	cups bell pepper, chopped	3	14½-ounce cans chicken broth
½	cup fresh parsley, chopped	1	8-ounce bottle clam juice
10	cloves garlic, minced		Salt, black pepper & cayenne pepper, to taste
1	cup celery, chopped	1	cup heavy cream
2	8-ounce cans tomatoes, crushed		

In a large heavy sauce pan, melt 1 stick of butter. Sauté all the vegetables except the garlic & tomatoes until translucent. Add broth & clam juice. Cook down to half of original volume. Add tomatoes, crawfish & garlic. Make a roux with the remaining butter & flour being careful not to burn. Stir roux into mixture to thicken. Add cream & remove from heat. Add salt & pepper. Serve hot.

Note: For variety, 2 pounds raw (small or medium) shrimp can be used instead of or in addition to crawfish. Either way it is wonderful.

Shrimp & Angel Hair Pasta

3	tablespoons olive oil	1	clove garlic, minced
1	bunch green onions, finely chopped	3	tablespoons basil, fresh & chopped
1	pound shrimp, raw & peeled	8	ounces angel hair pasta, cooked

Heat oil in skillet. Sauté onions 1-2 minutes. Add minced garlic and chopped basil. After 1 minute add the shrimp & cook until done. Add cooked pasta and mix thoroughly. Serve with tossed green salad & hot bread.

Nannie's Deviled Crab

3	tablespoons butter		2	eggs, hard boiled & chopped
3	tablespoons flour		1	pound crab meat, lump or
1¼	cup milk			pieces, picked clean of shells
3	heaping tablespoons ketchup		10	Ritz Crackers, approximately Salt & pepper, to taste
3	heaping tablespoons Worcestershire			Butter

In medium sized skillet: Mix butter & flour and add milk. Stir until smooth. Add ketchup & Worcestershire. Add chopped eggs and mix. Add crab & mix. Salt & pepper, to taste. Heat thoroughly. Put in greased Pyrex casserole, top with crumbled Ritz Crackers. Dab with small pieces of butter. Heat in 350° oven for 20 minutes. Be careful not to get cracker crumbs too brown.

Grilled Shrimp

3	pounds shrimp (65-70) without heads, peeled & deveined		½	cup dried oregano
			1	tablespoon cracked pepper
			1	tablespoon onion powder
2	cups olive oil		1	cup sea salt
1	teaspoon cayenne pepper		1	teaspoon garlic powder
½	cup dried parsley		1	tablespoon Tabasco

Mix ingredients together & marinate shrimp for 1 hour. Grill for 3 minutes on each side.

Seafood Sauce

2	cups mayonnaise		½	cup parsley, chopped
½	cup lemon juice		½	cup cilantro, chopped
1	tablespoon Lawry's Seasoned Salt		2	cloves garlic, minced
			2	tablespoons lemon zest
1	tablespoon cracked pepper		2	tablespoons orange peel
½	cup yellow pepper, chopped			

Stir together & serve in a chilled bowl.

Salmon Croquettes

2	14-ounce cans salmon	1	cup milk
	Juice of 2 lemons	2	egg yolks, beaten
1	small onion, grated	¼	cup milk
1	tablespoon worcestershire sauce	2	eggs
	Tabasco, several shakes	2	tablespoons oil
	Salt & pepper, to taste	3	tablespoons flour
3	tablespoons flour		Progresso Plain Bread Crumbs, enough to roll all croquettes
3	tablespoons butter or margarine	1	potato, peeled & boiled

Bone salmon and season with lemon juice, grated onion, Worcestershire, Tabasco, salt & pepper. Set aside. Make cream sauce with 3 tablespoons of butter, flour & 1 cup of milk. Add the 2 egg yolks beaten with ¼ cup of milk. Take off stove when the sauce begins to boil. Let cool for 5 minutes. Fold in the seasoned salmon. Put in bowl and when cool, refrigerate for at least 1 hour. To make croquettes, dip into 2 eggs beaten with 2 tablespoons of oil, roll in flour, then bread crumbs. Fry croquettes in hot grease for 5 minutes on each side or until golden brown.

William's Baked Dolphin

Mahi Mahi fillets **Mayonnaise**
Dijon mustard **White wine**

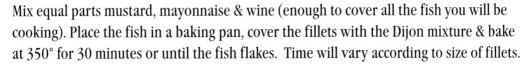

Mix equal parts mustard, mayonnaise & wine (enough to cover all the fish you will be cooking). Place the fish in a baking pan, cover the fillets with the Dijon mixture & bake at 350° for 30 minutes or until the fish flakes. Time will vary according to size of fillets.

Note: Dijon mixture comes out like a cheese sauce. It is very, very good.

Galveston Bay Gumbo

6	pieces chicken	1	tablespoons liquid crab boil
2	onions, choped	½	cup fresh dill, chopped (if
5	celery stalks, chopped		available)
2	bell peppers, chopped	2	quarts fish stock or water
4	cloves garlic, minced		Shrimp, oysters & crab, to
1	stick butter		taste
½	cup flour	1	tablespoon salt
16	ounces frozen or fresh okra,	1	teaspoon Áccent
	chopped	1	teaspoon red pepper
1	8-ounce can tomato sauce	1	teaspoon black pepper
1	10-ounce can Rotel tomatoes	2	tablespoons filé

Brown chicken in 2 tablespoons oil in a large heavy pot. Add butter & flour to make a dark roux. Use medium to low heat & watch carefully to keep from burning. Add water, chicken, okra, onions, bell pepper, celery, garlic, tomato sauce, Rotel tomatoes & seasonings, including filé, dill & crab boil. Bone chicken when tender & continue simmering until all vegetables are also tender. Usually a total of about 2 hours. Add seafood & cook 20 minutes more. Serve over rice. Add more filé or Tabasco if desired. Add a little sugar for an improved taste.

Note: Stock needed should be made from boiling shrimp & crab shells.

Cliffe's Dynamite Shrimp

1	pound medium shrimp	1	thin slice bacon for each shrimp
6-8	jalapeño peppers		Dash cayenne pepper
½	cup Worcestershire		Black pepper, to taste

Peel, clean & slice shrimp in half, leaving barely connected. Slice jalapeños in half or quarters & remove seeds. Place a strip of jalapeño in each shrimp. Wrap with slice of bacon & fasten with small skewers or toothpicks. Place on platter & sprinkle with pepper & Worcestershire sauce. Grill over hot coals.

Doc's Tiki Oven Broiled Shrimp

6	pounds shrimp in shells, uncooked	1½	pounds butter, not margarine
	Salt & pepper, to taste		French bread

Use a very large pan, so shrimp do not cover one another. Melt butter in pan. Put shrimp in melted butter & soak thoroughly on each side by turning over at least twice. Have broiler hot; salt & pepper until pepper is covering shrimp. Broil on 1 side for 7-10 minutes or until pink. Turn shrimp over & salt & pepper other side. Broil 7-10 minutes on this side also. When done, pour into large bowl for serving. Serve in individual bowls, giving each serving ample amount of butter for dipping French bread. Also, give each person an extra plate for shrimp shells. It is fun to give each guest a bib because this can be a little messy. But, it sure is good. Serve 5-8.

Shrimp A La King

1½	pounds shrimp, fresh or frozen	¼	cup flour
¼	cup butter or margarine	3	cups milk
½	green pepper, cut in strips	1	pimiento, cut in strips
¼	pound mushrooms, sliced	1	teaspoon Worcestershire
			Salt & pepper, to taste

Shell & devein shrimp. Cook in boiling salted water 3-5 minutes, until shrimp are pink & drain. Melt butter, add green pepper & mushrooms & cook until soft. Remove from heat. Add flour & stir until smooth. Return to heat & cook until bubbly. Add milk gradually, stirring constantly until thickened & boiling. Remove from heat. Blend in pimiento, Worcestershire sauce, salt & pepper. Add drained hot shrimp. Serve on split buttered English muffins, buttered toast or in toasted bread cups.

William's Spicy Crawfish Boil

140	pounds crawfish		Crawfish, Crab & Shrimp Boil
60	quart pot ½ full of water	10	lemons, juice only
1	bottle Louisiana Crawfish, Crab & Shrimp Boil	1	5-ounce bottle Tabasco
		1½	tablespoons salt
¼	cup Tony Chachere's Seasoning	⅓	cup pepper
		1	onion, chopped
⅓	cup cayenne pepper	1	5-pound bag new potatoes
1	bag Zatarain's Crawfish & Shrimp Boil	12	ears of corn, halved
		4	long links Venison sausage
2	4½-pound bags Louisiana	4	cloves garlic, whole

Makes about 140 pounds of crawfish. Cook approximately 35-40 pounds of crawfish at a time, boiling for 10-15 minutes each time. Serves a crowd.

William's Fish Tacos

If you can filet & fry it, you can use it for fish tacos! Best fish are firm, white-meated fish such as calico bass, freshwater bass, crappie, saltwater trout, redfish, flounder or snapper. If you're a catfish lover, go for it.

Check fillets for bones & remove any red veins. Wash, pat dry & refrigerate until ready to cook. Can be marinted in Lawry's Mesquite Marinade to add flavor. Prepare bowls of diced tomatoes, grated Cheddar or Jack cheese, and salsa. Sour cream, black olives & chopped lettuce are optional. Heat ¼" oil in frying pan. Mix 1 cup flour, ½ teaspoon salt, ¼ teaspoon pepper, ¼ teaspoon garlic powder on a paper towel. Coat fish fillet on both sides, then shake off excess flour. Lay gently into hot oil & fry quickly, turning once. Remove from pan & drain on paper towel. Fish may also be deep fried, but don't over-cook. While fish is frying, heat tortillas according to package directions.

Serve on counter or buffet style (paper plates & bibs are good). Each diner lays fish & condiments into warm buttered tortillas, rolling & folding tortillas into envelope style. Serve with Spanish Rice, made earlier from packaged mix and open a can of Ranch Style Beans. Zap 'em in the microwave.

William's Red Snapper

4	red snapper fillets	1	teaspoon oregano
1	teaspoon salt	2	ripe tomatoes, sliced ¼" thick
¼	cup lemon juice		
2	tablespoons olive oil	1	tablespoon fresh parsley, chopped
1½	teaspoons garlic, minced		

Preheat oven to 400°. Pat fillets dry & salt & pepper to taste. Mix lemon juice, olive oil, garlic & oregano in a small mixing bowl. Pour half into a shallow baking dish and lay fillets in mix, sides touching. Pour rest of mix over the fillets. Place the tomato slices over the fillets & place the dish in the oven for 12 minutes to cook. Serve at once.

William's Blackened Fish

This recipe works well with a number of different fish. My favorites are with grouper or tuna steaks on the grill, but it can certainly be used with catfish, trout, redfish. Just panfry with a little bit of margarine. Combine the following on a plate:

½	tablespoon paprika	¼	tablespoon garlic powder
¼	tablespoon cayenne pepper	¼	tablespoon black pepper
¼	tablespoon thyme		

You can play with the ingredients a great deal depending on the mood, adding white pepper or onion flakes. Lay fish on the mixture on the plate & flip to coat both sides. If the fish is dry, either rinse with a little water or spray a bit of non-stick spray. Then rub the mixture into both sides of the fish. Now you can either throw the fish on the grill or in a pan & cook roughly 5-10 minutes per side (depends on thickness of fish). Fish should be firm, but not hard when done. The grill is better because it helps sear in the juices, leaving a really tender fish when done. ***Bon Apetit!***

Shrimp Salad

5	pounds large shrimp		Salt & pepper, to taste
8-10	stalks celery, finely chop	2	green onions, minced
1	bag crab boil		

Fill large pot with water, bring to a boil, and add 1 bag of crab-shrimp boil. Add shrimp & boil for 7 minutes. Drain. Cut shrimp into bite-size pieces. Add celery and minced onions. Salt & pepper, to taste. Toss with Green Sauce (see below) until totally coated.

Green Sauce

1	pint sour cream	1	teaspoon horseradish
1	4-ounce jar Gerber's baby spinach	½	small onion, grated
	Juice of 1 lemon		Salt & pepper, to taste

Mix all ingredients thoughtly. Let stand for 3-4 hours. Especially good on crabmeat, shrimp or any fish.

William's Redfish on the Half-Shell

½	teaspoon salt & pepper, on each fillet	¼	teaspoon Worcestershire on each fillet
½	teaspoon Tony Chachere's, on each fillet	4	teaspoons oyster sauce, on each fillet
3-4	lemons		Butter, to taste

Fillet fish & leave skin on. This will allow you to put it directly on the grill over the fire. Apply seasonings to each fillet & squeeze lemon over them also. Top with Worcestershire added to oyster sauce. The amount really depends on the size of each piece. Place skin side down on the grill. Cook 15-20 minutes depending on size of fillets.

Note: Fish can be topped with sautéd onions & mushrooms for a delightful dish.

Stephen & Matthew's River Fry

4	fresh fish, skinned & fileted		1	cup corn meal, yellow
1	cup lemon juice		½	cup Masa Harina
1	quart canola oil		2	teaspoons salt
2	tablespoons paprika		1	teaspoon black pepper
	Dash red pepper		1	teaspoon dry mustard
1	cup corn meal, white			

Cut fish filets into finger strips. Put in container, cover with lemon juice & let sit for a few hours. Combine dry ingredients in a bag & mix well. Heat oil. Drop finger strips into dry mix, coat well & put into hot oil. Serve with Tabasco, ketchup & tartar sauce (see page 74).

Note: Oil is hot when you can drop half a lemon in & it floats to the top. Or more fun, drop in a match & it will light.

Lisa's Fish Fillets

2	tablespoons onion, finely chopped		1	teaspoon salt
			4	teaspoons pepper
1	medium carrot, cleaned & chopped		1-1½	pounds fish fillets
			1	cup dry white wine
1	lemon sliced		2	tablespoons Vermouth
	Pinch of thyme		1	tablespoon parsley, chopped
1	small bay leaf			

Heat oven to 400 °. Place onion, carrot, lemon, thyme, bay leaf, salt & pepper in a greased shallow baking dish. Place filets on top of vegetables. Combine wine & Vermouth & pour over fish. Bake 20 minutes or until fish flakes easily when pierced with fork. Sprinkle with parsley & serve with juices in baking dish. Serves 4.

Scampi Alla Margarita

2 pounds medium to large shrimp, shelled & deveined
¼ cup olive oil
1 large yellow onion, diced
4-6 large cloves garlic, minced
2 28-ounce cans Italian tomatoes, chopped
½ cup dry white wine, optional
½ teaspoon oregano, dried

Pinch thyme, dried
1 tablespoon fresh parsley, chopped
½ teaspoon sea salt
Pinch red pepper flakes, crushed
¾ teaspoon black pepper, freshly ground

Heat olive oil in a large sauce pan over medium heat. Add onion & Sauté about 4 minutes. Add garlic & continue cooking 3 more minutes, stirring occasionally. Add tomatoes & all their juices. Cook for about 25 minutes, stirring occasionally. Much of the liquid will be reduced. Add shrimp & wine to skillet. Add oregano, thyme, parsley, salt & both peppers & simmer for 4-5 minutes. Do not overcook the shrimp! Serve on a bed of al dente pasta. Serve 6-8.

Ceviche de Isla

2 pounds fish filets, very fresh only
1 cup lemon or lime juice, fresh squeezed
2 jalapeño peppers, chopped
½ cup onion, finely chopped

1-2 tomatoes, finely chopped
¼-½ cup cilantro, chopped (optional)
1 teaspoon salt
1 teaspoon pepper, white or black

Cut fish into bite-size pieces & place in glass container. Combine remaining ingredients. Cover fish with marinade. Let "cook" in refrigerator for at least 24 hours. Serve with tortilla chips or crackers as a dip, or stuff into avocado and serve as a salad. The lime juice cooks the fish–it isn't raw!

Note: Always remove seeds & membranes from jalapeño peppers if you don't like very spicy food. Chopped avocado may also be added just before serving.

Clara Paley's Shrimp Gumbo Bolivar Beach

2	pounds medium shrimp, peeled & deveined	½	teaspoon white pepper	
1	pound crabmeat	½	teaspoon cayenne pepper	
2	cups onions, chopped	½	teaspoon black pepper	
1½	cups green bell peppers, chopped	½	teaspoon thyme leaves	
1½	cups celery, chopped	½	teaspoon oregano leaves	
		¾	cup vegetable oil	
		¾	cup all-purpose flour	
		1	tablespoon garlic, minced	
		5½	cups basic seafood stock	

Seasoning Mix:
2   whole bay leaves
2   teaspoons salt

Combine onions, bell peppers & celery, & set aside. Combine seasoning mix ingredients well & set aside. Heat oil in large, heavy skillet over high heat until it begins to smoke, approximately 5 minutes. Gradually add flour, whisking constantly. Continue cooking, whisking constantly until roux is dark red-brown, about 2-4 minutes. Be careful not to let it scorch. Immediately add half of the vegetables & stir well. Continue stirring & cooking about 1 minute. Add remaining veggies. Continue to stir & cook 2 more minutes. Stir in the seasoning mixture & cook 2 more minutes. Add garlic, stir well & cook 1 more minute. Remove from heat. Place seafood stock in a large stockpot & bring to boil. Add roux mixture by spoonfuls to the boiling stock, stirring & dissolving it. Simmer this mixture for 10 minutes, & add shrimp & crabmeat. Return to a boil over high heat for a few minutes before serving. Serve over plenty of steaming hot rice. Serves 10.

Maggie's Grilled Tuna Steaks

4	medium size tuna steaks		2	cloves garlic, minced
¼	cup olive oil		1	teaspoon salt
2	tablespoons fresh lemon juice			Fresh ground black pepper, to taste
¼	cup scallions			
1	tablespoon fresh thyme leaves			

Whisk all ingredients except tuna steaks in a bowl until smooth. Pour over tuna steaks & let marinate for at least 1½ hours. Prepare a hot fire & grill them up! Cooking time will vary according to thickness and desirability of doneness, but generally about 5-6 minutes per side.

Vince's Avocado & Shrimp PoBoy

2	loaves of American French bread, cut in half		1	stick butter
1	pound shrimp, 40-60 count		3	cloves garlic, minced
3	avocados, sliced thin		1	bag Cheddar cheese, grated
½	cup cilantro, chopped		1	16-ounce jar Jardine's Cilantro Salsa

Peel, devein & cook shrimp. Combine butter, garlic & cilantro. Heat until butter is melted. Evenly spread mixture over halves of bread. Place sliced avocado on top of butter mixture. Place shrimp on top of avocado. Spoon salsa sauce on top & spread cheese over everything. Lightly put a touch of cilantro over all. Lay flat on cookie sheet & bake at 450° for 10 minutes until cheese is melted. Serves 6-8.

Birds & Stuffings

Birds & Stuffings

Preceding Page: The Whilden, Magness, and Halverson Families

Top row, left to right: Mary Elizabeth, Jay, Binford, Whilden & Bobby.

Bottom row, left to right: Robert III, Carol Grothues, Bobby, Mary, Bin, Margie, John & Lisa.

Our love and blessings go out to our friends and family who have loved and given so many blessings to us during our lifetime. Especially this last year. Thank you for being there for us and also for sharing your recipes to help with our newest cookbook, Cuckoo 2000!

John's Delicious Doves

24	doves
1	whole canned jalapeños
1	large onion
2	packages bacon

Marinade Sauce:

2	large bottles Italian dressing
12	ounces picante sauce
5	ounces Worcestershire
5	dashes Tabasco

Mix marinade sauce and set aside.

Clean doves and cut meat from breast bone. Chop onion into small pieces (size of breast meat), slice jalapeños the same way. Place one slice jalapeño, one slice onion in between 2 pieces of dove meat. Wrap with 1 bacon slice and secure with toothpick. Repeat until all dove meat is prepared. Place in marinade sauce and refrigerate overnight. Cook next day on grill for 15 minutes.

Jay's Nothing-In-The-Cupboard Chicken

4	chicken breasts	1	can ranch style beans

Preheat oven to 350°. Place chicken in a long casserole pan. Pour ranch beans over chicken. Cover with foil. Cook for 40 minutes.

Lauren's Baked Chicken

1	whole chicken	1	teaspoon butter
3	lemons		Lemon pepper Seasoning,
1	garlic clove		to taste

To prepare chicken, wash well and set in a glass casserole dish. Cut lemons & squeeze juice onto chicken. Place garlic cloves under skin all over chicken. Sprinkle with lemon pepper all over. Melt butter & brush chicken. Bake at 350° for 40-60 minutes until done.

Chubby's Barbecued Chicken Wings

24	chicken wings	1	small bottle Lea & Perrins
2	sticks of butter		Worcestershire
	Juice of 2 medium lemons	1	teaspoon salt
2	shakes soy sauce	½	cup vinegar

Melt butter & combine with lemon juice & Worcestershire sauce. Add soy sauce, salt & vinegar. Make fire in round barbecue bucket with wadded-up newspaper. It will take several pieces of paper wadded tightly. Light fire & place chicken wings between a double-sided wire rack with a handle & clip that holds handle together. As you turn the wings from side to side, brush on the sauce as they cook. They will look almost burned, but they are crispy & tasty. This is a "Down South" way to do chicken wings.

Note: To cook in the oven, marinate all day in sauce mixture. Place in shallow pan & broil at 500° until very brown. Turn & repeat. Reduce heat to 200° & cook for another 2 hours.

Lemon Herb Chicken with Dark Beer

1	whole 2½-3 pound chicken, split in half	1	tablespoon dried rosemary
		1	tablespoon tarragon
1	tablespoon Worcestershire	1	12-ounce can dark beer, any kind
1	tablespoon lemon zest		
1	tablespoon lemon juice		Salt & pepper, to taste

Coat chicken halves with all ingredients. Pour beer into shallow pan. Place chicken halves in pan. Cook uncovered 2½-3 hours (that's right) at 250°. Start basting after the first hour. This chicken will be crunchy yet fall apart.

Willie Dean's Dressing

9-10 cups chicken stock or broth
3 pans cooked cornbread
1 small loaf bread, dry
8 eggs
1 whole garlic bulb, peel pods
2 bunches celery, peeled & minced
4 jalapeño peppers, seeded & minced

6-8 bunches green onions, cleaned & chopped
2 green peppers, seeded & minced
4 white onions, chopped
1 stick butter
Salt & pepper to taste

Cook cornbread. Cool & crumble cornbread into a large bowl. Tear bread into small pieces & add to cornbread. Sprinkle 1 teaspoon black pepper over mixture. Sauté garlic in butter until soft & mash with fork. Add celery, onions & peppers. Cook until tender. Add 4 cups of stock to bread mixture & mix with electric beaters until smooth. Add broth until mixture is sticky, but slightly runny. Add eggs & mix well. Pour dressing into a pan or large skillet with cooked vegetables, stir to mix in vegetables, and cook until a little drier. Add more broth until right consistancy to put into pan or turkey. Let cool & refrigerate until ready to use or stuff turkey. In a pan, bake at 350° for 45-50 minutes. If used as turkey stuffing, stuff turkey right before you cook the bird.

Note: Recipe will stuff one large turkey & still have enough to fill a 13½x9x2½" Pyrex dish too.

Cajun Fried Turkey

1	10 to 12-pound turkey, remove giblets	2	gallons cooking oil, minimum
1	pound butter		
3	tablespoons Cajun seasoned salt		

Utensils Needed:
Meat injector, outdoor propane cooker, 10-gallon pot

Melt butter & blend in seasoning salt. Inject turkey with mixture all over bird. You will need a way to remove the bird from the hot oil if you don't have a large enough frying basket. To do this, take a coat hanger & wire the legs together, leaving enough wire to make a handle. Heat oil until drop of water pops on the surface. Submerge bird in oil. Cook 3 minutes for every pound plus an additional 3 minutes at the end. Remove from oil & place on surface to drain. The recipe applies to whole chickens as well.

CAUTION: *Because of the large quantity of oil & the use of the outdoor propane tank, this can be very dangerous. Let oil cool completely before discarding.*

Hunt, Texas Thanksgiving Dressing

1	dozen corn tamales	6	stalks celery, well peeled
1	16-ounce can cream corn	2	cloves garlic
1	10-ounce bag tortilla chips	2	cups chicken broth or turkey stock
3	beaten eggs		Cilantro, chopped (optional)
2	teaspoons oil		Salt & pepper, to taste
1	large onion or 1 bunch green onions, chopped		
1	jalapeño pepper, chopped		

Sauté celery, onion, garlic & jalapeño in oil until soft. Mash tamales with 1 cup of the stock. Add sautéed mixture, corn & eggs. Mix well until dressing consistency desired, adding more broth if necessary. Add seasonings & taste. Put crumbled tortilla chips in casserole, top with existing mixture & mash with a potato masher. Bake at 350° for 45-60 minutes. Don't let it dry out. A little jalapeño jelly instead of cranberry sauce is a fun change.

Chicken Willie

Step One

1	whole fryer
1	medium onion, whole
2	stalks celery, whole
	Salt & pepper, to taste
4	cups water

Stuff cleaned fryer with onion & celery. Place in water to cover. Add salt & pepper & cook with giblets until tender. Cook, debone, remove giblets & cut meat into chunks. Set aside.

Step Two

2	cups converted rice
4	cups water
1	teaspoon salt
2	10-ounce packages broccoli, chopped

Bring water & salt to a boil. Add rice and cook for 15 minutes, covered on high. Turn off & let set for 20 minutes. Cook broccoli as directed on package & drain. Combine with rice. Set aside.

Step Three

2	tablespoons butter
1½	cups onion, chopped
1½	cups celery, chopped
½	teaspoon white pepper
1	green chili, fresh & chopped
4	slices jalapeño pepper
2	cans cream of mushroom soup
1	can cream of chicken soup
1¼	cups sliced water chestnuts
	Dash of Tabasco, to taste
1	cup grated cheddar cheese
½	cup grated cheese, for topping

Sauté onion & celery in butter until tender. Combine all ingredients in Step Three. Add Step Two ingredients and cut up cooked chicken. Place in 15x10" Pyrex dish & top with another ½ cup of cheddar cheese. Bake at 350° for 35-40 minutes. Serves 6 to 8.

Maggie's Chicken Enchiladas

2   10-ounce cans Green Chili
    Enchilada Sauce
2   8-ounce cans tomato sauce
4   cups fresh chicken stock
1   10-ounce can Rotel
    Tomatoes, diced
1   2½-3 pound chicken, whole
2   pods garlic
1   onion, quartered
2   chicken boullion cubes
3   8-ounce bags Kraft Mexican
    Grated cheese
1   can green chilies, chopped
2   bunches green onions,
    chopped
2   packages tortillas, corn
    and/or flour

Place chicken in a pot, cover with water & add garlic & onion. Boil until tender. Let cool & debone, cube or shred. Set aside. Cook enchilada sauce, tomato sauce, tomatoes & chicken stock on low about 20 minutes. Set aside. Mix together 1 bag of cheese, chilies & 1 bunch of green onions for filling. Microwave tortillas in bag for 2 minutes to soften. Fill each with chicken & cheese mixture. Roll and place in 13x9x2" Pyrex dish (will fill 2). Put in refrigerator until ready to serve or freeze. When ready to cook, put ½ of sauce on each Pyrex to cover enchiladas. Top with remaining green onions & cheese. Bake at 350° for 20 minutes or until bubbly.

Emily's Broiled Chicken Breasts

Chicken breasts, boneless &
skinless
Lemon juice
Pepper
Dijon Mustard

Season chicken breasts with pepper & lemon juice. Place under broiler for several minutes. Turn and spread each breast with Dijon Mustard. Chicken will be tender to fork when it is done.

Shelley's Chicken Enchiladas

1	2½-3 pound chicken, whole	1	10½-ounce can Rotel Diced Tomatoes & Green Chilies
2	stalks celery, chopped		
2	chicken boullion cubes	1	cup chicken stock
	Seasoning salt, to taste	¾	cup green onion, chopped
1	small onion, quartered	7-10	flour tortillas
2	cups cheese, shredded		
1	10½-ounce can cream of chicken soup		

Place chicken in pot, cover with water & add celery, onion, boullion & seasoning salt. Boil until tender. Cool, debone & shred chicken. Reserve 1 cup of stock. Mix soup, Rotel & broth together & set aside. Combine chicken, green onions, half the cheese & 1/2 cup sauce in a bowl to make the mixture to fill tortillas. Heat tortillas in the bag 2 minutes in microwave to soften. Roll chicken mixture in tortillas placing seam down in 9x12" Pyrex dish. Pour remaining sauce on top & shake pan to settle sauce. Bake 20-30 minutes at 350°. Top with remaining cheese and let melt.

Chicken Cheese Crepes

	Crepes	¾	cup heavy cream
2	pounds chicken breast, cooked & diced	5	ounces green chilies, chopped
1¼	pounds Baby Swiss cheese, grated		Salt & pepper, to taste

Use homemade or store bought frozen crepes, thawed. Reserve 1 cup of grated cheese. Combine chicken, cheese, chilies, salt & pepper. Place a large spoonful of chicken mixture on each crepe & roll up. Place filled, rolled crepes in a shallow ungreased baking dish & top with reserved cheese. Pour cream over all. Bake at 325° for 20-30 minutes or until thoroughly heated.

Note: These may be frozen without cream topping. Thaw & add cream just before baking. Either Cheddar or Monterey Jack cheese can be used.

Chicken Nicholas

8	chicken breasts, boneless	Italian style bread crumbs
3	eggs, beaten	Salt & pepper, to taste

Pound chicken breasts until thin. Soak breasts in eggs; roll in bread crumbs. Sauté in melted butter until golden brown. Salt and pepper to taste. Kids love this dish.

Laurie's Easy Grilled Chicken

6	chicken breasts, boneless & skinless		Worcestershire Pic-A-Peppa
1	bottle Italian dressing	1	can Rotel Tomatoes

Place chicken in casserole dish. Put about 3 drops of Worcestershire and Pick-A-Peppa on each side of chicken breasts. Spread Rotel tomatoes across top. Cover all with dressing (about ½ bottle). Let sit ½ hour or longer. This is best if cooked over coals on bar-b-que pit, but it can be cooked on an indoor grill.

Willie Mae's Fried Chicken

1	Cut-up chicken	All purpose flour
	Salt & pepper, to taste	Wesson or Crisco Oil

Willie Mae is famous for her fried chicken. She swears there is no great secret to it, so maybe it's all "touch & timing". Wash chicken & cut off excess fat & skin. Drain. Salt & pepper both sides. Shake pieces in a bag of flour to coat.

Heat oil to 350-365°. Cook on one side until golden brown. Turn & brown on the other side. If one side begins to brown too fast, lower the heat. Drain chicken well on paper towels.

Dottie B's Chicken Spaghetti

3	packages spaghetti (1 pound)	3	cans tomatoes
3	large hens	1	pound butter
1	large can mushrooms		Parsley
1	pound sharp cheese	4	slices bacon
	Garlic	4	cups chicken stock
5-6	large onions		Tabasco
1½	large stalks celery		Celery salt
1	bell pepper		Salt & pepper, to taste

Cook hens in pot with seasonings as desired. Add onions, celery, salt & pepper. Chop bacon fine & brown. Add a lump of butter. Brown onions and garlic. Add bell pepper, parsley and tomatoes. Simmer with 4 cups chicken stock for 3 hours. Season with Tabasco, celery salt, salt and pepper. Add celery, mushrooms, and pieces of cooked chicken, plus more butter. Simmer 1 hour. Boil spaghetti. Add to sauce with grated cheese. Serves 25. This recipes may easily be cut into thirds.

Sarah's Doves in Wine

24	doves	2	cups red wine
	Salt & pepper, to taste	¼	cup vinegar
	Flour	¼	cup Worcestershire
1	cup butter		

Sprinkle doves with salt & pepper & lightly dust with flour. Brown in butter. Add other ingredients. Cook, in large covered skillet, very slowly for 1 hour. Thicken pan juices with flour & serve with doves.

Chicken with Ham & Cheese

1   chicken breast per guest, pounded thin

1   thin slice smoked ham per chicken breast

1   slice Swiss cheese per chicken breast
     Rosemary

Pepper
Butter, cut into tiny chunks

In three separate containers put:
flour
egg, beaten (1 per chicken breast)
bread crumbs, Italian style

Pound the chicken breasts thin. Put several tiny chunks of butter per breast. Sprinkle with pepper and rosemary. Place smoked ham and cheese slice on each chicken breast and roll up. Coat with flour, beaten egg and finally bread crumbs. Bake in oven at 375° for 30-40 minutes.

Chicken in Marsala Wine

1   chicken breast per guest, pounded thin

¼   cup butter per breast

¼   cup flour per breast

Salt & pepper, to taste

¼   cup Marsala Cooking Wine, per breast (Holland House Brand)

Pound the chicken breasts thin. Add salt & pepper to flour and roll the chicken breast in the flour. Add butter to a heated pan and let it get hot without burning. Pan fry the chicken breasts until done being careful not to burn. Remove the chicken breasts. Add the cooking wine to the pan and let the sauce boil and thicken. Add back the chicken breasts and serve together.

Note: Serve with Rice Pilaf–(Near East brand out of a box is good). Add a side of green vegetables like asparagus or green beans to complete meal.

Creamed Chicken

1 boiled hen, cut into 1" pieces
2 tablespoons flour
2 tablespoons butter
1½ cup milk (use ½ chicken broth if you have it)
3 shakes paprika
3 shakes Worcestershire
   Salt, to taste

Fresh cracked pepper, to taste

Boiled Chicken:

2 stalks celery, with leaves
1 green onion with leaf or regular sliced onion
2 cloves garlic
   Salt & pepper, to taste
3-4 cups water

Boil hen in large pot with 3-4 cups of water (about ⅓ of pot). Add 2 stalk of celery with leaves, 1 green onion with leaf or regular sliced onion, 2 cloves of garlic, salt & pepper and cook covered for about 2 hours or until wing moves easily. Debone & cut up chicken. Make a cream sauce using flour, butter and milk. Add seasonings to taste. Place cut up chicken in sauce and cook until well mixed. Serve over rice.

Susan's Cornbread Dressing

Cornbread:
½ cup flour
1 cup white corn meal
1 teaspoon baking powder
½ teaspoon baking soda
1 teaspoon salt
2 tablespoons sugar
1 cup buttermilk
1 egg
2 tablespoons cooking oil

Sift dry ingredients. Add milk, egg and oil. Mix well. Bake at 400° in 9" hot greased heavy skillet or pan. Cool after baking.

Dressing:
In skillet sauté in butter:

2 bunches green onions, chopped
2 green bell peppers, chopped
1 bunch celery, chopped

Add to crumbled cornbread in large mixing bowl.

Add:
1 package Pepperige Farms stuffing mix
4-5 cans chicken broth, one at a time until desired consistency. (Not too dry or too soupy.)

Bake in casserole at 350° until hot throughout.

Turkey Stuffing

¾-1¼   cup chicken or turkey stock
2   cups cornbread
6   cups day old whole wheat bread
2   eggs
¾   cup butter, melted
½   teaspoon sage
½   teaspoon thyme
½   teaspoon marjoram
1   teaspoon salt
1   apple, diced & unpeeled
⅓   cup onion, finely minced
½   cup celery, finely minced (inner stalks with leaves)
    Pecan halves, use several handfuls

Make stock early in the week. This is very important for delicious turkey stuffing but if an emergency arises, buy Swanson's clear chicken broth. Make cornbread. I use Pioneer mix, but use your own favorite recipe. Crumble cornbread & dried bread into small cubes. (Leave crust on bread). Beat eggs until foamy and stir in melted butter and seasonings. Use large mixing bowl or roaster to combine breads, diced apple, onion, celery and pecans. Add beaten eggs and seasoning mixture. Stir well. Begin adding stock and test carefully after you have added about ¾ cup. Mix with hands. When dressing holds together and barely separates as you lift it with a fork, you have added the right amount of stock. Refrigerate. Follow directions in the turkey recipe for baking instructions.

Note: Bread can be placed in a low or warm oven to slightly dry it out. This can take several hours

Turkey Stock

1   chicken neck, gizzard, heart
2   celery, stalks with leaves
1   carrot
1   onion, chopped
1   teaspoon salt
1   bay leaf
    Peppercorns
6   cups water

Put the above ingredients in a large pot and bring to a boil. Reduce heat to simmer. Cover and simmer as long as you can up to 5 hours. Strain & refrigerate.

Turkey Paste

4	tablespoons butter	2	tablespoons lemon juice
5	tablespoons flour		Dash cayenne pepper

Cream these ingredients together until you have a smooth paste. Rub breast and wings & all parts well in this paste. This keeps the bird moist. Do not put on too thickly.

Turkey

There is a warm happy feeling when your turkey turns out golden brown and juicy on the inside. If you follow these steps, you will have just that.

1. Be sure the turkey is perfectly clean the morning before you cook it. Remove all spongy portions along ribs and back bone, rinsing in cold water.

2. Using paper towels, pat the inside and outside of your turkey dry. Rub lightly inside with salt. Wrap in waxed paper and place in refrigerator.

3. Prepare the "Turkey Stuffing" and stuff turkey when the filling is cold, preferably the night before. Don't overstuff. Allow for swelling. Skewer neck & body skin over cavities, this is important.

4. Before baking, cover lightly with "Turkey Paste" & place on rack breast side up. Cover with foil and begin roasting. (We fix the turkey the day before, turkey paste, stuffing etc., cover with foil & refrigerate until ready to bake.)

5. Preheat oven to 500°. Place turkey in 500° oven for 20 minutes. Reduce heat to 250-275° (depending on your oven). For an 18-20 pound turkey, bake for 2 hours with foil on. Then remove the foil and continue to cook. Bake approximately 4 hours. Turkey is ready when the leg moves slightly.

6. Allow approximately 25 minutes per pound for an 8-pound turkey, 20 minutes per pound for a 12 pound turkey and 12-15 minutes for a 20-pound turkey.

Mexican Chicken Casserole

6   chicken breasts, skinless
1   dozen corn tortillas
1   cup milk
1   can green chili salsa
1   10½-ounce can cream of
     mushroom soup

1   10½-ounce can cream of
     chicken soup
1   medium onion, grated
1   pound cheddar cheese, grated

Bake chicken at 400° for 1 hour. Bone, skin & cut into pieces. Cut tortillas into 1"
strips. Butter large baking dish & cover with half of the tortillas. Then add half the
chicken pieces. Mix soups together with milk, onion & salsa. Pour half of the mixture
over tortillas and chicken. Then make another layer using the remaining tortillas &
chicken. Pour the remaining soup mixture over this layer. Cover with cheese. Bake at
350° for 45 minutes or until firm (but not too brown). Serves 4.

Ola's Baked Chicken

1   or 2 whole chickens, cut in
     half
     Seasoned salt

Lemon pepper
Áccent
Garlic salt

Pat chickens dry. Season with above ingredients, to taste. Put in foil pan, breast up.
Cook in 350° oven until golden brown & turn over. Cook until this side is brown also.
Cook one hour. Cover with foil, turn oven off & leave until ready to eat.

Easy Chicken Breast Parmesan

4	chicken breasts, boneless, skinless, cut in half	1	cup Parmesan cheese, grated
1	cup Italian bread crumbs	1	stick butter or margarine, melted

Pound chicken pieces with mallet between waxed paper or Saran wrap. Combine bread crumbs & Parmesan cheese. Dip chicken pieces into melted butter & dredge in bread crumb mixture. Place chicken on greased cookie sheet. Bake at 350° for 30-40 minutes.

Chicken & Rice Casserole

1	whole chicken, boiled & deboned	2	10½-ounce cans cream of mushroom soup
1	package wild rice	1	package Pepperidge Farm Herb Seasoned Stuffing
1	pound pan sausage		
2	medium onions, chopped	1	stick butter or margarine

Cut cooked chicken into bite-size pieces. Brown sausage in skillet & save drippings. Sauté onions in drippings. Prepare rice as directed, using chicken stock instead of water. In a large bowl, combine chicken, sausage, onions, rice & soup. Transfer into greased casserole dish after mixing. In a skillet, melt butter & sauté stuffing mix. Top the casserole with bread crumbs. Bake 30 minutes at 350°. Serves 8.

Hunter's Fine Duck

12	wild ducks		***Blend:***	
1	cup Blend		½	cup salt
1	10-ounce bottle Heinz 57		¼	cup black pepper
2	sticks butter		⅛	cup red pepper
1	onion, minced		⅛	cup celery salt
8-12	garlic pods, minced			
	Water			

Combine Blend ingredients & add onions & garlic. Add this to Heinz 57 sauce. Wash & clean ducks. Rub mixture on ducks, inside & out. Put ducks in baking pan & pour remaining sauce over. Add water to pan to half cover the ducks. Dot with butter. Bake at 350° for 1 hour, uncovered. Cover & bake another 1½ hours. Add water if it cooks down too far. Baste frequently.

Note: You may use bacon strips instead of butter to top the ducks before cooking.

El Rey's Grilled Dove

8-12	doves		3	green onions, chopped
⅔	cup soy sauce		1	stick margarine or butter, melted
¼	cup sherry			
⅔	cup water		1½	tablespoon Tabasco
½	teaspoon garlic powder		2	tablespoons Worchestershire

Combine, soy sauce, sherry, water, garlic powder & green onions. Place the doves in marinade for 3-4 hours. For sauce, combine margarine or butter, Tabasco & Worchestershire sauce. Grill dove outside over low heat. Baste with sauce, not Marinade. Grill until tender, time will vary. The slower the grilling the more tender the doves.

Margaret's Grilled Quail

8	quail	1½	cups apricot preserves
1	cup Worchestershire		Salt & pepper, to taste
1	cup Italian dressing	4	fresh cloves garlic
2-3	dashes teriyaki sauce		

Rinse the quail and rub them with the pressed garlic cloves. Add salt & pepper & let sit while you blend the Worchestershire sauce, Italian dressing and teriyaki sauce. Pour this mixture over the quail in a snug fitting pan with sides to it. Spoon out the apricot preserves covering the quail inside & out as best you can. Let them marinate at least an hour or two before grilling them on a medium fire. The apricot preserves create a wonderful glaze as the quail grill on the fire.

Note: Try apple jelly, orange marmalade or red currant jelly, too. Try putting some fresh jalapeño peppers or peppered bacon inside the birds.

Christiana's Chicken Fajitas

½	cup lemon or lime juice (about 6 lemons)	6	tablespoons cilantro, chopped
6	tablespoons olive oil	1	tablespoon garlic, chopped
2	pounds chicken breasts, boneless & skinless	1	jalapeño, chopped
			Salt & pepper, to taste

Mix all the ingredients except the chicken breasts to make the marinade. Put chicken breasts in glass bowl & pour on marinade. Let marinate for at least 2 hours, or overnight. Grill over hot coals and slice into strips.

Glenda's Easy Baked Chicken Kiev

½   cup butter
4   teaspoons chives, chopped
½   teaspoon thyme
⅛   teaspoon ground pepper
2   whole chicken breasts, deboned, skinned, halved & pounded

Flour to dust
1   egg
1   teaspoon water
1½   cups any stuffing mix
4   tablespoons butter, melted

Combine butter, chives, thyme, & pepper. Form into 4 rectangles & freeze in waxed paper. Then place 1 frozen rectangle in middle of each chicken breast & fold chicken so the butter is enveloped. Dust with flour. Slightly beat egg with 1 teaspoon water. Dip dusted chicken breasts in egg wash and roll in stuffing mixture. Pat well & chill 1 hour. Place on cookie sheet & drizzle with butter. Bake at 375° for 20 minutes.

Sterling's Marinated Quail

12   quail
12   slices bacon
2   12-ounce cans jalapeños, juice only

1   16-ounce bottle La Martinique True French Vinaigrette
1   16-ounce bottle Seven Seas Viva Italian dressing
     Fiesta Brand Fajita Seasoning

Make a tray of heavy duty foil or use 9x13" glass casserole dish. Wrap each quail in bacon & secure with toothpick. Lay quail in tray. Sprinkle with fajita seasoning. Combine the 2 dressings & jalapeño juice & pour over quail. Marinate 4-6 hours. Do not drain marinade. Cover with foil & cook on grill over medium coals 15-20 minutes. Serves 4-6.

Meats, Gravies & Sauces

Meats, Gravies & Sauces

Preceding Page: The Allen Family
Left to right: Jenny, Jessica, Nancy, Kendall, & Morgan.

John's Easiest Venison

1   or more venison backstrap
     steaks
1   large bottle Italian dressing

1   5-ounce bottle Worcestershire
3-4 dashes Tabasco

Pound venison steaks out, but not too thin; just enough to tenderize. Marinate in above ingredients 6-8 hours or overnight. Cook over grill approximately 5 minutes each side.

Lisa's Shish-Ka-Bob Over Rice

Beef or chicken strips
Bell pepper
Pearl onions
Mushrooms

Cherry tomatoes
1   bottle Ranch Dressing
1   bottle Italian Parmesan
     dressing

Prepare skewers alternating ingredients and marinate in dressing, the longer the better. Place on top of foil to grill. Salt and pepper, to taste. Serve over rice.

Gayla Cyr's Pork Tenderloin

1   pork tenderloin
1   chopped onion
1   can Mission Style Jalapeños,
     finely chopped

6   pieces maple flavored bacon
     Lawry's Herb & Garlic Liquid
     Marinade
3-4 tablespoons Worcestershire

Marinate tenderloin in marinade mixed with Worcestershire sauce. Split tenderloin down center & stuff with onions and jalapeños, to taste. Wrap bacon around tenderloin & secure with toothpicks. No meat should be showing. Cook on top shelf of grill, wrapped in foil for 45 minutes. Leave on warm grill for 30-45 minutes.

Parker's Spicy Pot Roast

3½-4½	pounds chuck roast		5	garlic pods, peeled & crushed
½	cup oil		1	stick butter
3	tablespoons flour, heaping		1	large onion, sliced
3	tablespoons soy sauce		5	carrots, sliced
1	tablespoon Tabasco Habanero		1	10½-ounce can beef broth
1	35-ounce can tomatoes, crushed		2	cups water
			1	tablespoon granulated sugar

Preheat oven to 350°. Salt & pepper roast. Heat oil in Creuset pot or Dutch oven. Brown roast on top & bottom 2 minutes. Brown all sides 1½ minutes each & set aside. Add butter to pot & melt. Add carrots & onion. Cook for 2 minutes. Add flour & stir until carrots & onions are coated. Add water & beef broth & stir slowly. Add tomatoes, garlic pods, soy sauce, Tabasco & sugar. Bring to a simmer & put roast back into pot. Cover & put into oven for 1 hour. Take out & turn roast. Cook another hour & turn again. Lower heat to 250° & cook another 30 minutes. Remove roast from pan & set aside. Remove vegetables & cover with foil. Bring juices to a boil on top of the stove. Reduce until a desired thickness is obtained, stirring frequently for about 8-10 minutes. Carve roast and place back in reduced sauce. Serve hot.

Ginny's Quick Barbecued Brisket

With a sharp knife remove all the visible fat from the brisket. Rub meat with favorite seasoning salt. I prefer Cajun variety. Cook brisket 3 hours on your favorite pit at 250-300° with plenty of smoke. Remove the brisket and wrap in heavy foil. Double seal foil. Place back on grill & continue to cook 3 more hours at 250°. Brisket will fall apart and have a nice smoke ring for the traditionalists.

Note: The reason it takes most people 12-16 hours to barbecue a brisket is because they have to cook off 3" of fat. We advise you cut off this fat. It is the fat in the center of the meat which makes it tender, not the fat on the outside.

P's Death by Ribeye

4	1¼-inch ribeye steaks		3	tablespoons Guy's seasoning
2	cups extra virgin olive oil		2	tablespoons crushed black
10	garlic pods, crushed			Pepper

Place steaks on a carving board & tenderize with a meat cleaver or hammer until ¾ inch thick. Poke holes in the tenderized steaks with a fork. Rub Guy's seasoning & pepper into steak, pressing seasoning into meat. Place steaks into glass dish & thoroughly coat with oil. Then rub crushed garlic all over steaks. Cover dish with plastic wrap & place in refrigerator. Marinate for 4 hours or more. Steaks must be cooked over a very hot, charcoal or gas grill. Cook 3-4 minutes a side for medium rare to medium. Eat immediately.

Note: Steaks are not for the weak hearted watching their cholesterol. To increase calories, mix melted butter into the olive oil & apply to steaks.

Faunty's Meat Loaf

1	pound ground hamburger or turkey meat		1	teaspoon fresh ground black pepper
1	onion, minced		2	tablespoons fresh cilantro, chopped
2	slices white or dark bread			
1	8-ounce can tomato sauce		⅓	cup Cheddar cheese, grated for topping
2	cloves fresh garlic			

Break meat into small pieces in a bowl. Run bread under water faucet to soak, then squeeze dry. Work into meat. Add spices, and ⅓ can of tomato sauce. Form loaf. Put 1 can of water around loaf & cook at 375° for 30 minutes. Pour remaining tomato sauce over meat. Cook at 350° for 30 more minutes. Cover & let sit until ready to serve.

Note: Just before serving top with grated cheese & place under broiler at 400° for 5 minutes.

Leftover Mexican Idea

If you have taco meat, enchiladas, chili con queso or beans left over, layer the ingredients you have & top with freshly grated Cheddar cheese. Freeze & thaw for another great meal. Serve on toasted tortillas & top with guacamole salad after cooking. Makes a divine casserole.

Fran's Enchiladas

1 pound ground meat	2 teaspoons cumin
1 onion, chopped	1 package corn tortillas
1 clove garlic, minced	1 2-pound can any good chili
2 jalapeño peppers, minced	Pace Picante sauce
1 teaspoon Lawry's Seasoned Pepper	Grated Cheddar or Rat cheese

Brown ground meat & add onion, peppers, garlic & spices. Cook until done. Put soft tortillas into hot oil for 1 minute. Remove & drain. Put tortillas in bowl of picante sauce, turn on both sides & remove. Fill each tortilla with 2-3 tablespoons of meat mixture. Roll & place in a 3-quart casserole flat dish. Repeat until all tortillas are filled. Cover with chili & top with grated cheese & chopped onion. Cook 30 minutes in 350° oven or until bubbly. Serves 6.

Gloria's Flour Tortilla Enchiladas

1½	pounds ground beef	1	pound Cheddar cheese, grated
2	10½-ounce cans cream of chicken soup	8	ounces sour cream
		¼	cup onions, chopped
1	4-ounce can green chilies with juice, chopped	20	flour tortillas

In large skillet, brown beef, drain the fat & set aside. In large pan combine undiluted soup, chilies, half the cheese, sour cream & half the onions. Stir in three-fourths of the ground meat. Cook over medium heat until well-mixed & thickened. Preheat oven to 350°. Spoon 2 tablespoons sauce mixture into each tortilla, rolling them up & placing them side-by-side in a 13x9x2" baking dish. Put remaining filled tortillas in smaller pan. Pour remaining sauce over rolled tortillas. Top with remaining onion, cheese & meat. Bake, uncovered, 30 minutes, or until bubbly. Makes 10-12 servings.

Note: Chopped chicken can be substituted for the ground beef.

Kay's Smoked Shoulder Clod

1	whole beef shoulder clod	Guy's Seasoning

Have butcher order this cut of meat in advance. Roll & tie whole shoulder clod. Rub it generously with Guy's Seasoning. Smoke slowly on a pit at opposite end of fire for 14-16 hours. Add more coals & hickory chips as needed. One shoulder clod will serve about 20 people as a main course, or a crowd at a cocktail party.

Note: For variation, prepare brisket in same manner. Smoke 5-6 hours.

Parker & Lara's Honey Mustard Pork *Tender* Loin

1	cup spicy mustard	1	teaspoon salt
1	cup honey	1	teaspoon pepper
¼	cup of fresh rosemary, chopped	2	1-pound pork tenderloins

Mix first 5 ingredients in bowl. Rub on tenderloins, covering liberally. Cover & place in refrigerator, and chill for a minimum of 30 minutes. Preheat oven to 400°. Place tenderloins in oven for 30-45 minutes until firm to touch, or the thermometer reads 160°. Let cool for 5 minutes, carve & serve hot.

Note: This recipe is great cooked on the grill. Do not cook over direct heat, but use the middle rack!

Serrano Pepper Bearnaise Sauce

2	egg yolks	1	tablespoon tarragon, dry
3	sticks salted butter		Juice of 1 lemon, medium
3-4	tablespoons serrano peppers, finely chopped	½	teaspoon tarragon vinegar, optional

In a mixing bowl, whip egg yolks & lemon juice with a whisk. Let stand 10 minutes. Heat butter until bubbling. To keep from burning, stir with whisk while melting & heating. Drizzle hot melted butter into egg yolk mixture, whisking continuously. Gently mix in peppers, dried tarragon & tarragon vinegar.

Note: Excellent over pork or beef tenderloin. Also great served with wild rice & green vegetables. Your favorite spicy pepper can be substituted for the Serrano peppers.

Robby's Smoked & Stuffed Pork Tenders

2   pork tenders, 1½-2 pounds of meat

1   pound frozen crawfish tail meat, cooked

½-¾   pound Mozzarella cheese, grated

1   poblano pepper, sliced thin

2-3   whole green onions

1   cup Italian salad dressing

     Cotton butchers string

With a very sharp knife cut down the midline of each tender almost the entire length. Press each side flat with your palm. Once again repeat the cut & press process with each half of tender created. The object is to create a flat piece of tender as thin as you can make it. To stuff, lay the green onions down the middle of one of the tenders & add poblano pepper. Next, mound the crawfish meat on top of peppers & onions. Place slices of Mozzarella on top of tails, down the length of the tender. Top with the second tender. Precut pieces about 10 pieces of string & tie tenders together the length of the whole piece. Be careful to stuff any protruding filling as you tie up the tenders. Marinate the stuffed & tied tenders in Italian dressing several hours before cooking. Cook on barbecue pit 2½-3 hours. If your pit has a thermometer, I suggest 225-250° for cooking. The tenders are done when they feel firm to the touch. Serve with Serrano Pepper Bernaise Sauce on page 114.

Note: Let stand 5-10 minutes & slice carefully to preserve the presentation of the stuffed medallions.

Bongie's Hunter's Mustard

1   4-ounce Coleman's dry mustard

1   cup vinegar

2   eggs beaten

1   cup sugar added to eggs

Combine mustard and vinegar in a jar overnight. Next morning add mustard and vinegar to the egg and sugar mixture. Cook over medium heat until thickened, stirring often. Add a pinch of salt. Serve with any meat.

Chicken Fried Venison

If you don't have a cast iron skillet you are wasting your time on this one! Trust me.

2   pounds your favorite cut of venison, sliced & tenderized (to tenderize meat, pound with a cleaver)

Salt & pepper, to taste

Cajun seasoned salt, to taste

Flour for dredging

2   eggs

3   cups milk

Oil for frying

Salt & pepper tenderized meat, to taste. Place flour & Cajun seasoning in a bag, shake together, & set aside. Beat together eggs & milk. Place meat in seasoned flour & coat all sides thoroughly. Take out & dredge in egg-milk wash. Place again in flour & coat thoroughly. Remove & fry in at least 2 inches of hot oil, turning until done. Serve with cream gravy.

Cream Gravy: After frying meat, pour off all oil except 3-4 tablespoons. Add 3-4 tablespoons unseasoned flour, & add salt & pepper, to taste. Stir constantly over low heat. When mixture is browned (very quickly) add 3-4 cups milk & stir over medium heat until it thickens. ***Yum!***

Luke's Fajita Marinade

1   pound butter

2   10-ounce bottles soy sauce

2   16-ounce bottles Wishbone Italian Dressing

1   10-ounce bottle Worchestershire

2   whole lemons, peeled & chopped

2   tomatoes, chopped

2   cloves garlic, crushed

2   15-ounce cans Rotel chiles & tomatoes

1   can beer or 1 cup Tequila, optional

Combine all ingredients and boil for 5-10 minutes. This will marinate 10 pounds of fajita meat. Marinate meat for 12-24 hours and grill over hot coals.

Marinated Venison

1	cup oil	½	cup vinegar
	Lawry's Seasoned Salt	¼	cup Lea & Perrins
	Pepper, to taste		Worcestershire
	Lawry's Garlic Salt	6	vension backstrap steaks

Combine first 6 ingredients to make marinade. Place marinade over steaks & leave for at least 6-8 hours, turning meat in marinade at least once every 2 hours. Cook on charcoal broiler as you would any steak. No wild taste to this deer meat!

Note: Venison is always better if cooked medium rare to medium.

Walter's Pork Tenders on the Grill

4	pork tenders	2	teaspoons Dijon Mustard
6	cloves garlic, mashed	⅓	cup lemon juice
2	tablespoons soy sauce	½	cup olive oil
2	tablespoons fresh ginger, grated		Salt & pepper, to taste
			Charcoal

Mix all ingredients & pour over pork tenders. Marinate pork tenders for 12 hours. Remove meat from the refrigerator & allow it to become room temperature. Grill about 6" from coals for about 20 minutes, turning on all sides.

Nancy Cooksey's Crock Pot Pork Chops

1-2	cans condensed chicken broth	½	teaspoon salt
4	extra thick pork chops	½	teaspoon garlic powder
½	cup flour	2	tablespoons oil
1½	teaspoons dry mustard		

Combine dry ingredients. Dredge pork chops in dry ingredients & brown in hot oil. Pour chicken broth over meat. Cook in crock pot for 2-4 hours.

Note: Two cans of chicken broth makes for more gravy.

Smoked Pork Loin

	Pork loin roast	2	tablespoons brown mustard (yellow mustard and brown sugar can be mixed if you do not have brown mustard)
	Rosemary		
	Pepper		
3	tablespoons soy sauce		
2	tablespoons White wine Worcestershire Sauce	3	pods garlic, crushed
			Charcoal & Hickory chips

Sprinkle pork loin generously with rosemary & pepper. Mix other ingredients; pour over the pork. Let stand in refrigerator for a couple of hours. Smoke on grill at opposite end from fire. Cook at very hot temperature with hickory chips for 30 minutes. Partially close vents on pit to lower temperature and cook for 2-3 hours until tender.

Note: This can be cooked in the oven for 15 minutes at 500° and lowered to 300° for 2-3 hours.

Pork Chop Casserole

4-6	medium thick pork chops	1	onion
1	cup rice	1	can consomme
1	tomato		Salt & pepper, to taste
1	bell pepper		

Sprinkle pork chops with salt and pepper. Brown on both sides in skillet. Sprinkle rice in bottom of casserole. Arrange pork chops on top. On top of each pork chop, place a slice of onion, bell pepper, and tomato. Pour consomme over all. Bake in 350° oven about 1½ hours, until pork chops are tender and rice has absorbed all the moisture. It may be necessary to add liquid. Do not pour consomme on casserole and let it sit before cooking.

Rib Roast

5-7 **pound rib roast**
Lemon pepper, to taste

Cracked pepper, to taste
Salt, to taste

Take roast out of refrigerator 2-3 hours before ready to cook. Sprinkle lemon pepper, cracked pepper and salt on roast. Bake uncovered in preheated 500° oven in mid afternoon for 30 minutes. Turn off but don't open oven door. Roast will be rare when dinner is ready.

Korean Bul-Go-Gi–Marinated Beef

1 **pound flank steak or rib eye steak, sliced thin**
2½ **tablespoons soy sauce**
2 **tablespoons water**

1 **tablespoon sugar**
1 **tablespoon sesame oil**
2 **cloves garlic, minced**
Black pepper, to taste

Mix the ingredients together for the marinade. Marinate beef for at least 1 hour. Best grilled but it could also be cooked in the oven. Serve with rice and red-tip lettuce by rolling meat and rice in the lettuce.

Margie's Easy Barbecue Sauce

1 **cup salad oil**
1 **cup onion, chopped**
1 **tablespoon dry mustard**
1 **cup ketchup**
1 **cup Worcestershire**

½ **cup white vinegar**
Juice of 2 lemons, reserve rinds
1 **teaspoon salt**
1 **teaspoon pepper**

Simmer onions & dry mustard in oil until onions are soft. Add remaining ingredients, including the lemon rinds. Simmer for 30 minutes. Stir occasionally. Discard lemon rinds and pour in large jar. Store in refrigerator.

Beef Stroganoff

1	pound boneless beef sirloin steak	1	teaspoon instant beef bouillon granules
1	cup fresh mushrooms, sliced	1½	cups water
4	tablespoons butter or margarine	¼	teaspoon dry mustard
½	cup onion, chopped	⅔	cup sour cream
2	cloves garlic, minced	4	tablespoons dry white wine
2	tablespoons ketchup	½	teaspoon salt
2	tablespoons all-purpose flour		Pepper, to taste
			Hot cooked noodles (I prefer the wide egg noddles)

Thinly slice the beef across the grain into bite size strips. In a skillet, brown the meat in 2 tablespoons of the butter or margarine. Remove meat. Add remaining 2 tablespoons of butter or margarine, mushrooms, onion and garlic to skillet. Cook until the onion is crisp-tender. Stir in the flour, ketchup, bouillon granules, mustard, salt & a dash of pepper. Add water. Cook & stir until thickened and bubbly. Cook and stir 2 minutes more. Stir in the beef strips. Stir in sour cream. Stir in the wine. Heat thoroughly but do NOT boil. Serve over noodles. Serves 4.

Rob's Green Peppercorn Sauce

4	14½-ounce cans beef broth	½	cup any dark liquor that isn't sweet (bourbon or cognac)
2-3	tablespoons green peppercorns, dry	1	stick butter
3	tablespoons chopped shallots	1½	cups heavy cream

Brown the shallots in butter. Add remaining ingredients except cream. Cook over medium heat until two thirds of original volume is gone. Add the cream and continue to cook mixture to sauce consistency. Stir frequently. Cooking time is about 1½ hours but it is worth the effort.

Note: Great on any red meat or wild game.

Laurie's Lasagna

1	pound ground beef	15	ounces Ricotta cheese
1½	cups water	½	cup Parmesan cheese
3	cups spaghetti sauce	2	eggs
	(homemade or 28-ounce jar)	½	teaspoon salt
2	cups Mozzerella cheese	¼	teaspoon pepper
	(reserve 1 cup to sprinkle on	1	8-ounce package of lasagna
	top)		noodles, uncooked

In saucepan, brown meat and drain excess fat. Add water, spaghetti sauce and simmer about 15 minutes. In a bowl, mix together Ricotta cheese, eggs, Parmesan cheese, half of Mozzarella cheese, salt & pepper. Pour 1 cup of spaghetti sauce mixture on bottom of 9x13x2" baking dish. Arrange 3 uncooked lasagna pieces lengthwise over sauce, cover with about 1 cup of spaghetti sauce mixture. Spread half of cheese mixture over the sauce. Repeat layers of lasagna, sauce and cheese mixtures. Top with layer of lasagna, and remaining sauce. Sprinkle remaining Mozzarella cheese on top. Cover with foil. Bake at 350° for 45 minutes, remove foil and bake and additional 15 minutes. Let cool approximately 15 minutes before cutting. Makes 10-12 servings.

Papa Joe's Steak Sauce

½	cup butter	½	cup Dry Vermouth
½	cup catsup	1	4-ounce can mushrooms,
½	cup soy sauce		drained

Mix all ingredients together. Heat 5-10 minutes.

Note: This sauce is excellent on any kind of steak.

Roach Family Pot Roast

1	4 to 6-pound roast, rump preferred	3	potatoes, sliced 1" thick
½	cup flour	6	large cloves garlic, crushed
1-2	medium size onions, sliced	3	tablespoons olive oil
8	carrots, sliced		Salt & pepper, to taste
			Water

Roll roast in peppered flour until completely covered. Heat oil in a large heavy pot. Brown roast on all sides. Add approximately 1" of water into pot. Turn heat to low. Add garlic & onions, on & around roast. Salt can be added now. Cook covered about 4 hours. Check water level every 60 minutes. If water is needed to maintain 1" in depth around roast, keep adding it each time you check. Place sliced potatoes & carrots in juice around roast & cook 1 hour. Roast is ready when it falls apart with touch of a fork. Cannot be overcooked as long as water level is kept consistent.

Note: This roast generally takes about 1¼ hours per pound of meat to get to the desired doneness indicated in recipe.

Kate McConn's Beef Tender

1	beef tender, trimmed	Lawry's Seasoning Salt

Preheat oven to 500°. Rub beef all over with Lawry's. Cook for 20 minutes at 500°. Turn off oven & let meat stand in oven for 30 minutes. Do not open oven door. Beef will be pink in the center & brown on top.

Michelle's Schnitzel

10	thin slices veal, chicken, turkey or pork tender	1	cup flour
3	eggs, beaten	2	cups bread crumbs
	Paprika, salt & pepper, to taste	2	teaspoons water
			Oil for frying

Place meat between 2 pieces of waxed paper and pound thin with meat cleaver or heavy knife. Mix bread crumbs & seasonings in a flat pan. Put flour in another pan. Beat eggs well with water. Dip each meat slice in flour, then egg wash, then roll in bread crumbs. Place on flat sheet & refrigerate until time to cook. Pour 1" oil in large frying pan. Fry meat about 3-5 minutes or until golden brown & crisp.

Note: You may use part cracker crumbs instead of all bread crumbs.

Doug & Randa's Osso Bucco

1	cup flour	6	cloves garlic, crushed
1	teaspoon salt	1	cup tomatoes, peeled
¼	teaspoon pepper	1	cup white wine
4-5	veal shanks, cut into 2" pieces	1	teaspoon basil
3	tablespoons olive oil	1	teaspoon thyme
1½	cups onions, coarsely chopped	1	bay leaf
1	cup carrots, coarsely chopped	3	tablespoons fresh parsley
1	cup celery, coarsely chopped		

Combine flour, salt & pepper. Coat veal in mixture & shake off excess flour. Heat olive oil in a large, heavy pot. Sauté the veal, turning them until all sides are nicely browned. Remove from pot and set aside. Add onions, carrots, celery & garlic to the pot & sauté for about 5 minutes. Add coarsely chopped tomatoes, wine, basil, thyme & bay leave. Mix well & bring to a boil. Put the veal shanks back into the pot & cover. Simmer for about 2 hours. Just before serving add the chopped parsley.

Note: It is better to have the butcher cut veal shanks into the 2" pieces.

Reckling Boys Butterfly Lamb

1	5 to 6-pound leg of lamb, boned, butterflied & flattened	4	cloves garlic, minced	
1	cup olive oil	4	sprigs rosemary	
½	cup lemon juice	2	tablespoons soy sauce	
¼	cup red wine or vinegar	2	tablespoons Worcestershire	
	Fresh ground pepper & salt, to taste	½	teaspoon Tabasco	

Have butcher bone & butterfly lamb. Remove fat & skin. Flatten so it looks like a big steak. Mix all ingredients but pepper & rosemary. Marinate lamb 2 to 24 hours. Prepare charcoal grill. Place lamb on grill & sear both sides. Put on ground pepper & rosemary. Close grill top & cook 45-60 minutes.

Mark's Baseball Dogs

6	wieners	1	cup Cheddar cheese, grated	
6	strips bacon		*or*	
		1	can squirt cheese	

Split wieners. Stuff cheese down center. Wrap with strips of bacon. Place a toothpick to hold bacon on wiener. Bake at 350° until bacon is cooked through. Serve with bowls of mustard, ketchup & hot sauce for dipping. Can also be served on a bun with your favorite chili.

Pat's Hamburger Noodle Bake

1½	pound hamburger meat	½	pint sour cream	
2	small cans tomato sauce	1	cup rat cheese, grated	
1	onion, chopped	1	10-ounce package noodles	
1	8-ounce package cream cheese		Salt & pepper, to taste	

Brown ground meat & onion. Add tomato sauce & 1 can water, salt & pepper. Simmer 20 minutes. Cook noodles as directed on package. Mix cream cheese & sour cream together, making a soft consistency. Layer meat, noodles & sour cream mixture until all is gone. Top with grated cheese & bake for 30 minutes at 350°. Serves 8 generously.

Mama Galen's Meatballs

1	pound ground pork		1	teaspoon pepper
1	pound ground beef, lean		1	teaspoon salt
4-5	cloves garlic, crushed		1	teaspoon oregano, dried
2-3	small sour dough rolls, stale or hardened		3	tablespoons Italian parsley, chopped
2	eggs			Olive oil
4	tablespoons Romano cheese		1	clove garlic, slivered
1	teaspoon Lawry's Seasoned Salt			

Put stale or hardened sour dough rolls in blender to form bread crumbs. Mix all ingredients in a large bowl. Form meatballs 1" in diameter. Cover bottom of large skillet with olive oil & a few slivers of fresh garlic. Brown meatballs on all sides. Remove & drain on paper towels. Simmer in your favorite sauce for 4-5 hours. Serve over spaghetti or linguine.

Note: Use your own homemade recipe or tomato sauce that can be bought in jars.

César's Beef Tender

1	whole beef tenderloin, trimmed	Salt & pepper, to taste

Leave tenderloin at room temperature for one hour. Set oven to broil. Completely cover top of meat with salt & pepper. Place meat in the middle rack of oven. Broil for 25 minutes. Do not open door. Turn oven off & leave meat another 10 minutes, without opening the door. Remove & slice as desired.

Note: Timing is for medium-rare cooking. For medium-well, leave in turned-off oven an additional 10 minutes.

César's Pozole
Pork Stew

3-4	pound pork shoulder with bone	10	chilies cascabel, seeded
6-8	quarts of water	½	head cabbage, shredded
3	cloves garlic	1	bag tortilla chips
3	bay leaves		Salt, to taste
3	15-ounce cans of hominy		Lemon wedges

Boil pork, garlic & bay leaves in a very large pot with the cover on. Cook on medium heat for 2-3 hours. Check water level throughout & add more water as needed. To test doneness of pork, take a fork & poke the pork in the middle. If meat tears away from middle of the bone, it is done. If not, continue cooking until test works. Be careful not to overcook pork. When done, remove & place on a large platter.

In a separate saucepan, boil the chilies. Water will change color & chilies will be very soft when done. Place chilies & water from the pan in a blender. Remove the garlic cloves from the soup pot & put in the blender with the chilies mixture. Blend on high for about 5 minutes.

Trim excess fat from pork & cut into chunks. Return pork to the soup pot & add hominy. Pour chilies & garlic mixture through a colander (to avoid pepper skins) into the pot. Only use enough of the spicy mixture to color the water red. Bring the soup to a boil. Boil for about 20 minutes, uncovered. Add the other can of hominy & salt. Turn off burner & remove bay leaves. Serve in bowls & garnish with shredded cabbage, tortilla chips & lemon wedges.

Note: Chilies Cascabel are the long Mexican red peppers which are dried.

Veal Shanks

3	or 4 veal shanks (about 1½" thick)	1	16-ounce can Italian diced tomatoes
2	tablespoons olive oil	1	can chicken broth
1	small onion, chopped	½	can dry white wine
3	cloves garlic, crushed	1	tablespoon white wine vinegar
2	stalks celery, chopped	3	or 4 basil leaves
2	cups baby carrots		Fettucine noodles

Brown shanks in olive oil. Add remaining ingredients and bring to a boil. Reduce heat and simmer for 1-1½ hours, until veal is tender. Serve over fettucine noodles. Serves 3-4

Note: For leftovers, add a can of tuna to remaining sauce & serve over fusilli pasta.

Lorie Herod's Veal Scalopini

4	cups flour, more as needed	2	tablespoons olive oil
½	cup Parmesan cheese, grated	2	cloves garlic
1	teaspoon salt	½	cup dry wine, optional
⅛	teaspoon pepper	½	cup beef consummé or stock
1½	pounds veal cutlets or beef cube steaks	1	tablespoon lemon juice
			Parsley, chopped

Mix flour, cheese, salt & pepper together. Wipe meat dry, sprinkle with flour mixture & pound into meat with a meat tenderizer. Heat olive oil with garlic clove & brown meat lightly on both sides. Add wine, stock, lemon juice and 1 garlic clove. Cover & simmer 30-45 minutes. Sprinkle with parsley and serve.

Aunt Alice's Stuffed Meat Loaf

Combine 1 pound each:
> Ground beef
> Pork
> Veal

Add:
2   eggs, beaten
1   cup milk
1   tablespoon salt
1   teaspoon pepper

Mix well. Divide & put half in greased baking pan.

Stuffing:
3   cups bread crumbs, toasted
1   teaspoon salt
½   teaspoon thyme
⅛   teaspoon pepper
1   tablespoon onion, minced
2   tablespoons oil
1   cup canned mushrooms, chopped

Retain the liquid from mushrooms or stock to moisten. Mix all together & place on top of meat. Top with other half of meat. Bake in 350° oven 1½ hours. Serves 12.

Cissy Beeler's Chicken Fried Steak

> Wafer thin sirloin steaks
> Milk
2   eggs

Flour
Salt & pepper, to taste
Canola oil

Mix eggs with milk (enough to cover steaks) in Pyrex pan. Cut up steaks into individual sizes and put in milk. Let soak for about an hour in refrigerator. In largest Ziploc freezer bag put some flour, salt & pepper. Shake steaks in flour until well coated. Fry in heated oil in electric skillet until both sides are golden brown. Serve with cream gravy.

Cream Gravy: After all steaks have been fried & put onto a platter, pour excess oil from skillet. Add flour to skillet & whisk until light brown. Add milk & whisk until all lumps are out and it is the desired consistency. Salt & pepper, to taste.

Potatoes, Rice & Pasta

Potatoes, Rice & Pasta

Preceding Page: The Bruce Family
Top, left to right: Walter, Kay and Kirk Bruce; Elizabeth, Walt, Jr. and Walter Bruce;
Middle: Nicholas, Gib, Emily and Wilson Chapman; Bottom: Kirk, Thomas and Susan Bruce;
Laurie Bruce; Nicholas Chapman and Cy Bruce.

Betsy's Au Gratin Potatoes

6	medium potatoes, peeled sliced ¼ thick	2	dashes Tabasco
1½	cup Cheddar cheese, grated	¼	teaspoon white pepper
2	cups milk	¼	teaspoon cayenne pepper
4	tablespoons cornstarch	1	teaspoon paprika
½	teaspoon salt	½	stick margarine or butter

Boil potatoes in 4 cups of salted water. Cook 6 minutes only. Drain & set aside. Melt butter & add cornstarch until it bubbles. Add paprika, salt & white pepper. Gradually add milk & stir constantly until thickened. Remove & add grated cheese. Add Tabasco & cayenne pepper & set aside. In oblong Pyrex casserole, place potatoes evenly. Pour sauce over top. Cover with more grated cheese & cook at 350° for 20 minutes, or until it bubbles. Serves 10-12.

Note: Can be frozen before baking.

Garlic Potatoes

2	pounds small new potatoes, unpeeled	½	teaspoon salt
2	tablespoons olive oil	3	tablespoons basil or parsley, chopped
4	garlic cloves, minced		Pepper to taste

Heat oven to 350°. Cut potatoes in halves or quarters. Mix oil & garlic in baking dish. Add potatoes & toss to coat. Add salt & pepper. Bake about 1 hour, turning 3 times. Garnish with basil or parsley.

Yummy Potato Casserole

1	2-pound package frozen hash browns, thawed	1	10½-ounce can cream of chicken soup
1	8-ounce sour cream	1	cup onions, chopped or
1	cup milk	1	cup green onions, chopped
2-4	tablespoons butter		Salt & pepper, to taste
2	cups sharp cheddar cheese, shredded	2	cups bread crumbs or
		2	cups cornflakes, crushed

In a small saucepan, combine butter, milk, 1½ cup of cheese, cream of chicken soup, sour cream, onion, salt & pepper. Melt over medium heat until smooth. Place hash browns in a greased 9x13" casserole dish & pour melted mixture over top. Add remaining ½ cup of chedder chesse & top with bread crumbs. Bake at 350° for 1 hour.

CAUTION: It is extremely hot when you take it out of the oven. Very Yummy and full of fat! Don't use nonfat items because it isn't very good!

Lisa's Green Rice

3	cups cooked white rice	2	tablespoons olive oil
2½	cups milk	1	cup parsley, chopped
2	cups Sharp Cheddar cheese, grated	4	green onions, finely chopped
2	eggs beaten	1	tablespoon Worcestershire

Mix all, season to taste with salt and pepper and place in a greased casserole. Bake at 350° for 40 minutes.

Very Simple Potatoes

1   Idaho potato per guest,
    peeled & cut into large chunks

1   onion per guest, cut into large
    chunks or thick slices

Olive oil, enough to coat
potatoes & onions

Salt & pepper, to taste

Coat the potatoes & onions with generous amounts of olive oil, salt & pepper. Bake in 400-450° oven for approximately 40 minutes or until potatoes are definitely golden brown & onions are carmelized.

Note: For variety, you can use new potatoes.

Stuffed Potatoes

Baking potatoes
Milk
Butter
Salt & pepper, to taste

Sharp cheddar cheese
Sour cream or bacon bits, if
desired

Bake potatoes in 400° oven for about 1 hour. Split potatoes lengthwise and scoop potato from peeling. Add butter, salt, pepper and heated milk until mixture is a good consistency to restuff into potato shells. (Sour cream and bacon bits may be added with other ingredients, if desired.) Top with grated cheese. Just before serving, place in a 350° oven for about 20 minutes, until hot and the cheese is melted.

Nani's Candied Sweet Potatoes

4	large sweet potatoes	¼	teaspoon cinnamon
1	cup sugar	1	teaspoon vanilla
1	cup white Karo Syrup	½	cup pecans, chopped
2	tablespoons butter		

Peel potatoes & cut in chunks. Drop potatoes in water to cover and boil 15 minutes. Pour off most of water, leaving 1" with potatoes. Add syrup & sugar and lower heat to a low steady boil for 20 minutes to thicken. Add butter, cinnamon & vanilla. Continue to boil as it thickens. Add pecans. DO NOT STIR POTATOES. Remove from heat & serve.

Donna Maddox's Chicken Spaghetti

1	large fryer, for 2 cups chicken	1	can cream of chicken soup
3	tablespoons butter	1	4-ounce jar pimientos, chopped & drained
1	onion, chopped		
2	cloves garlic, crushed	1	jar mushrooms, sliced & drained
1	green pepper, chopped		
1	stalk celery, chopped	½	cup white wine
1	can cream of celery soup	1	pound Cheddar cheese, grated
1	can cream of mushroom soup		

Cook chicken in seasoned water; remove chicken and save stock to use in cooking spaghetti. Sauté onion, garlic, green pepper & celery in butter until translucent. Cook noodles in chicken stock until almost tender. Put in colander, drain & rinse in cold water. Mix all of the above ingredients with the noodles except the cheese. Spoon into shallow 9x13" baking dish. Top with grated cheese; sprinkle with paprika. Heat in 350° oven until bubbly & cheese is melted. Serves 10-12.

Risotto Francesca

3	tablespoons butter		Juice of ½ lemon
1	cup leeks or green onions, chopped	2	cups Arborio Italian Rice
4	cups chicken stock or broth	1	cup Parmesan cheese, grated Paprika

In a large skillet, melt 2 tablespoons butter. Add onion & lemon juice & sauté until tender. Add rice & braise on medium heat for 3 minutes, stirring constantly. Add a few dashes of paprika. Add stock, 1 cup at a time. Stir, cover, & cook for 10-15 minutes. Add remaining stock ½ cup at a time every 10 minutes until all broth is absorbed. Remove from heat, stir in cheese & remaining butter. Serve immediately. Serves 6-8.

Note: Yellow or red peppers can be substituted for the leeks & green onions, or a combination of all 4 may be used. Also a teaspoon of saffron in the broth gives it a new taste.

Baked Ziti

½	pound ziti macaroni	2	cups prepared spicy spaghetti sauce
1	pound Ricotta cheese		
3	cups Mozzarella cheese, grated	½	cup Parmesan cheese

Cook ziti as directed, and mix with Ricotta & Mozzarella cheeses. Grease 9x9" Pyrex dish. Cover bottom with spaghetti sauce. Add ziti mixture & cover with remaining spaghetti sauce. Sprinkle with Parmesan & ½ cup of Mozzarella cheeses. Bake at 350° for 25-30 minutes.

Mexican Chicken Spaghetti

1	large onion, chopped		2	10½-ounce cans cream of mushroom soup
1	2½-3 pound chicken, whole		2	10½-ounce cans cream of chicken soup
3	chicken boullion cubes		½-¾	cup chicken stock
2	16-ounce package Velveeta cheese		1	24-ounce package spaghetti, cooked
2	10-ounce cans Rotel Diced Tomatoes & Green Chilies		2	cups grated Cheddar cheese

Place chicken in pot & cover with water. Add onion & boullion cube & cook until tender. Let cool. Debone & cube chicken. Place in broth left over from boiling chicken so it will stay moist. Melt Velveeta & Rotel together. Add soups & chicken broth. Drain broth from chicken cubes. Layer spaghetti, chicken & sauce mixture in a 9x12" Pyrex dish. Bake at 350° for 30 minutes. Sprinkle Cheddar cheese on top & melt. Serves 6-8

Rigatoni with Bacon & Onion

2	tablespoons olive oil		3	ounces Campbell's Concentrated Beef Broth
½	large onion, sliced thin			
½	pound bacon, cut into small bits (Hickory or Mesquite smoked)		½	10-ounce can stewed tomatoes
				Pepper, to taste
				Parmesan cheese to top

Sauté onions in olive oil until the onions are soft. Add the bacon after you cut into small bits. After the bacon is cooked, add stewed tomatoes & beef broth. Pepper to taste. You don't need to add salt since the beef broth and bacon are already salty. Simmer for 15-20 minutes until the sauce thickens. It should not look watery.

Note: I serve this over Rigatoni, but penne or fusille is also good. The original recipe called for Prosciutto or Pancetta Italian Bacon.

Chinhui's Ragu Bolognese
Meat Sauce with Tomatoes

2	tablespoons olive oil
½	large onion
2	stalks celery
1	medium carrot
1-1¼	pound ground beef (see note)
1	carton Pomi Strained Tomatoes
	Or may substitute ¾ large
	can tomato puree

5-6	whole cloves
½	whole nutmeg
	Salt & pepper, to taste
	Parmesan cheese to top

Chop the vegetables very fine, as small as possible. Sauté in olive oil in medium sauce pan until vegetables wilt. Add the ground meat and brown. Stir in the meat to get rid of the lumps, this will make the sauce smooth. Add the tomato puree and salt and pepper to taste. Add the whole cloves and use a small spice grater to grate the nutmeg into the sauce. Simmer for 30-40 minutes. Do not forget to top with Parmesan cheese.

This sauce is simple but there are three "Musts" 1. You MUST vigorously stir the meat while it is browning so there are no lumps of meat in the sauce and the sauce is smooth. 2. You MUST make sure you add enough salt, otherwise the sauce does not come alive. 3. You MUST use whole nutmeg. You can substitute pre-ground nutmeg in a pinch, but it won't be as good.

Notes: Can substitute half ground veal and half ground beef. I usually serve this over penne pasta.

Spaghetti Carbonara

1	pound bacon, hickory smoked		Lots of pepper, to taste
3-4	egg yolks, beaten	½-⅔	cup Parmesan cheese, grated
			Spaghetti, cooked

Cook the bacon until crisp & save just a little bit of the grease. Set aside. Beat the egg yolks (I've been told the plainer folks use the whole egg but my high-brow friends pooh-poohed this) in a small bowl & add the pepper. The pepper & cheese are the key to this or otherwise it feels like you are spooning grease into your mouth. Do not be shy about adding pepper. I would start with ½ teaspoon & keep adding until I can't take it anymore. Add the grated Parmesan. The good Parmesan cheese like imported Regianno is really necessary for this dish.

Usually I like to mix the sauce & pasta before I serve. For this dish, it is a must. Once you cooked the spaghetti, drain, but do not rinse the pasta so it remains hot. Stir in egg & cheese mixture, adding a spoonful or two of the bacon grease you have reserved. If the pasta is too cooked, you might have to cheat & heat the whole thing over very low heat just a little bit. Top each dish with bits of cooked bacon. You might have to add salt to this dish, it just depends on the Parmesan cheese & bacon you use.

Jenny's Rice Balls

Rice, sticky short grained	Salt

Prepare plenty of sticky short grained rice like they serve in Japanese or Korean restaurants. Wash & wet your hands so the rice does not stick to them. Shape the rice into a ball your favorite size. Sprinkle with salt & enjoy.

Note: Chinese, Indian, Thai or Uncle Ben's rice will not work.

Macaroni & Cheese

¼	cup butter	1	cup Parmesan cheese
¼	cup flour	1	cup Peckorino
3½-4	cups milk	¼	cup Mascarpone
¼	cup Blue cheese	1	pinch nutmeg
1	cup Gruyere cheese, grated		Salt & pepper to taste
	Or Gorgonzola, Fontana or	1½	pound pasta, cooked
	Cheddar)		

Make roux with flour & butter (cook 1 minute). Gradually whisk in milk (it will break up the roux). Simmer for 15 minutes. Throw in cheese & seasonings. Simmer until melted. Pour into cooked pasta. Serve hot.

Note: You can bake this, more like lasagna. Top with grated Parmesan cheese & bake at 350° for 30 minutes.

Jessica's Macaroni & Cheese, Pepperoni Rollups

1	box Kraft Deluxe Macaroni & Cheese	1	teaspoon salt
		1	tablespoon oil
1	package pepperoni, large thin slices		

Following directions on box, bring your water to a boil & add salt & oil to water. (Eddie says this is what makes satisfying macaroni & cheese). Cook macaroni as directed, then drain & rinse. Add cheese as directed. When finished, place macaroni & cheese in the middle of a large thin slice of pepperoni & roll up like a burrito.

Sarah's Herb Rice

8-10	slices bacon		1	cup celery, chopped
3	tablespoons bacon drippings		2½	cups rice, cooked
1	small onion, chopped		2	tablespoons soy sauce
1	cup canned mushrooms, sliced		1	egg, beaten

Fry bacon, crumble & set aside. Sauté onion & celery in bacon drippings. Add mushrooms, cooked rice & soy sauce. Before serving, reheat & stir in beaten egg & crumbled bacon. Makes 6 servings.

Rice with Mushrooms

1	cup rice		½	cup white wine
½	onion, chopped		2	tablespoons Parmesan cheese
1	13-ounce can chicken broth		2	tablespoons butter
12	fresh mushrooms, sliced			

Melt 1 tablespoon butter & sauté onions until soft for about 5 minutes. Add mushrooms & wine. Cook until wine is evaporated. Add rice & cook until well coated with butter. Add broth & bring to a boil. Cover tightly. Reduce heat to low & cook for 20 minutes without peeking. When ready to serve, toss rice with Parmesan cheese & butter.

Poppi's Pasta

1	16-ounce package penne pasta		2	tomatoes, peeled & chopped
1	container pesto, homemade or Contadina		1	8-ounce package Feta cheese, crumbled

Boil pasta according to directions. Drain well. Add pesto sauce & feta cheese. Toss in tomatoes. Serve warm or great as a cold pasta.

Curry & Dill Pasta with Chicken or Shrimp

1   12-ounce package Garden Twirl Pasta
1   4-ounce jar pimentos, chopped
1   4-ounce jar black olives, chopped
1   cup mayonnaise
1½ cups celery, chopped
1   small red onion, chopped
1   bell red or yellow pepper, chopped
2   teaspoons curry powder

1   tablespoon dill
    Salt & pepper, to taste
    Pasta

Marinade:
½   cup salad oil
¼   cup lemon juice

Variations:
    Sliced chicken breasts
    Boiled shrimp

Cook pasta according to directions. Soak pasta in marinade overnight in covered container. If it isn't possible for you to soak overnight, soak at least 6 hours. Add all other ingredients & let set approximately 4-6 more hours.

Sweet Potato Casserole

3½ pounds sweet potatoes
2½ sticks butter or margarine, softened
2   medium eggs
¼   cup milk
1½ teaspoon pumpkin pie spice
    Dash salt, nutmeg, cinnamon & ginger

1   teaspoon vanilla extract

Topping:
1½ sticks butter or margarine, softened
1½ cups brown sugar
¾   cup flour
2   cups pecans, chopped

Peel & cook potatoes on top of stove until soft. Place in large bowl & add remaining ingredients. Mix & pour into a lightly buttered baking dish. Add topping & bake at 350° for 25-30 minutes. To make topping, mix margarine or butter and brown sugar. Add flour & mix thoroughly. Add pecans & spread over top of casserole.

Matt's Macaroni & Cheese

1   7-ounce package macaroni, elbow or shells

2   cups cottage cheese, small curd

1   cup sour cream

1   egg, slightly beaten

¾   teaspoon salt

     Pepper, to taste

1   8-ounce package Cracker Barrel Sharp cheese, shredded

Cook macaroni according to package directions. Drain well. Combine cottage cheese, sour cream, egg, salt & pepper. Add shredded cheese, mixing well. Stir in cooked macaroni. Grease 9x9x2" baking dish. Put macaroni mixture in dish & bake at 350° for 45 minutes. Serves 6-8.

Mary Elizabeth's Pronto Penne Pasta

1   medium package penne pasta

½   cup chopped onion

2   cloves garlic, chopped

2   tablespoons butter

½   pound ground meat

1   jar Classico, Fire Roasted Tomato & Garlic Marinara Sauce

Cook pasta, drain and put aside. In large skillet, add butter and sauté garlic and onions. Add meat and brown. Add marinara sauce and bring to a low boil. Cover & simmer 15 minutes. Add pasta and mix until all pasta is coated evenly. Serve 6-8.

Louise Brollier's Spaghetti Sauce

2	green bell peppers, chopped	1	cup water
3-4	ribs celery, chopped	2	tablespoons salt
1	large yellow onion, chopped	1½	teaspoons pepper
½	cup vegetable oil	1	teaspoon sugar
3	pounds ground beef	3	tablespoons fresh basil, chopped
3	cloves garlic, minced		
2	15-ounce cans diced tomatoes	3	tablespoons fresh oregano, chopped
3	15-ounce cans tomato sauce		
2	12-ounce cans tomato paste	1	cup Italian parsley, chopped

Sauté bell pepper, celery & onions in oil in a large pot until soft. Add ground beef & garlic. Brown. Add remaining ingredients. Simmer 2 hours. Serve over cooked spaghetti. Freezes well.

Luc's Rice Dressing

Cook 1½ cups rice until partially done & dry. Add rice to dressing just before serving. Cook 5-10 minutes. It will absorb water. This is the last cooking.

Dressing:

3	pounds pork fat
	Giblets from fowl
½	cup lard or Crisco
⅔	cup flour for roux
2	cups onions, chopped
1½	cups celery, chopped
2	cups bell pepper

Cook in large iron skillet, Crisco and flour to make a roux. Cook until browned. Separately cook remaining ingredients in another skillet until done, about 20 minutes. Add to roux.

Add:

1	cup parsley, chopped
1	pint oysters, whole
3	cups water

This mixture should boil 10-15 minutes before adding to remainder of dressing. *Note: For onions, use 1 cup each of white and green onions.*

Liz Spradling's Paella

6	cups chicken broth	1	small jar pimientos, minced
½	teaspoon saffron	1	pound medium shrimp, shelled
1	small onion, peeled	3	cups Arborio Rice (Uncle Ben's
12	chicken thighs		okay)
	Sea salt, to taste	5	tablespoons parsley, chopped
½	cup olive oil	2	bay leaves, crumbled
10	Goya Chorizos, sliced (Fiesta)	½	cup dry white wine
1	large butterfly pork chop, diced	1	tablespoon lemon juice
¼	pound Prosciutto ham, diced	¼	pound frozen peas
1	large onion, diced		24 clams, small
4	scallions, chopped	18	mussels
4	cloves garlic, minced		Lemons for garnish

Heat the broth with the saffron & whole onion. Cover & simmer for 15 minutes. Remove onion & measure the broth you will need exactly to 5½ cups. Wash & dry chicken, sprinkle with salt. In a metal paella pan, with a 15" base, heat the oil. Add the chicken & fry over high heat until golden. Remove to a platter and once cooled, debone. Drain most of the oil & chicken juices from pan. Add the chorizo, pork and prociutto to the pan and stir fry about 10 minutes. Add the onion, scallions, garlic & pimientos and sauté until onion is wilted. Add the shrimp until it turns pink & remove it to chicken platter. Add the rice and stir to coat it well with the oil in the pan. Sprinkle in parsley and bay leaf. Stir in the chicken broth (boiling hot), wine, lemon juice & peas. Bring to a boil & cook uncovered & stirring occasionally over medium-high heat for 10 minutes. Bury the shrimp & chicken in the rice. Add the clams and mussels, pushing them into the rice, with the edge that will open face up. Bake at 325° uncovered for 20 minutes. Remove from oven once rice has soaked up all liquid but is still moist. Cover loosely with foil for about 10 minutes. Decorate with lemon wedges. Serve with French bread & red wine.

Note: Soak clams & mussels in 3 gallons of water and 3 tablespoons of cornmeal the day before in the refrigerator.

Dorothy Paterson's Lasagna

1	large jar of Ragu spaghetti sauce	1½	cup onion, chopped
1	8-ounce package lasagna noodles	2-3	bricks Mozzarella cheese, grated
1	16-ounce carton small curd cottage cheese	1	cup Parmesan cheese
1	egg	1½	pounds ground beef
			Salt & pepper, to taste

Brown meat with chopped onion. Drain off fat. Add salt & pepper. Add Ragu Sauce. Simmer together for 30 minutes. Allow meat mixture to cool. Cook noodles in large pot. Mix Parmesan & Mozzarella cheeses. Mix cottage cheese with egg. Layer in a Pyrex dish in the order of noodles, meat mixture, cottage cheese/egg mixture & cheese mixture. Repeat the layering 2 more times, in the same order. Generously sprinkle with remaining Parmesan & Mozzarella mixture. Bake at 325° for 45 minutes, or until bubbly hot.

Chow Mein Rice

1	cup brown rice	1	green pepper, chopped
1	pound hot sausage	1	onion, chopped
1	can cream of chicken soup plus water to make 1 quart of liquid	4	stalks celery, chopped
		1	small package almonds, sliced
			Corn flakes to cover top

Cook sausage until well done. Add chopped onions, green pepper, celery & soupy liquid. Simmer 5 minutes. Add raw rice & almonds. Pour in large loaf pan. Bake 1 hour at 350° for 30 minutes. Before done, add corn flakes to top & continue baking until done.

Robert's Fried Rice

2	tablespoons olive oil		3	tablespoons soy sauce
1	bunch green onions, chopped (include some of green tops)			Salt
1	cup celery, diced			Chopped, blanched almonds, browned in butter
2	cups cooked white rice			

Sauté onions and celery in oil but do not brown. Add rice, salt and soy sauce. Mix and place in casserole. Bake at 350° for 30 minutes. Toss almonds on top just before serving.

Note: For a different taste, we sometimes add cooked, cut-up shrimp, chicken or beef before cooking.

César's Rice-Broccoli Casserole

1	cup white rice, cooked		1	medium white onion, chopped
1	small package Velveeta cheese		1	10½-ounce can cream of mushroom soup
1	10-ounce package chopped broccoli, frozen			
1	stick butter			

Melt the butter in a large skillet. Reduce heat to medium high. Add chopped onions & sauté until translucent. Add the broccoli & cook until tender. Add cream of mushroom soup & cook for about 3 minutes. Add half of Velveeta cheese cut into small chunks. Cook until cheese is melted & add cooked rice. Add remainder of of the cheese chunks & cook until cheese has melted. Place in large baking dish & cook at 350° until top starts bubbling.

Ann McCarroll's Fettucine

10	grilled chicken strips & sausage links	1	pint Half & Half cream
1½	cups butter	1	pound Velveeta Cheese, cut into pieces
3	medium onions, chopped	2	cloves garlic, chopped
2	medium bell peppers, finely chopped		Salt & pepper, to taste
¼	cup all purpose flour	1	pound fine fettucine noodles, cooked
4	tablespoons dried parsley		

Melt butter in large saucepan. Add onions & bell peppers and cook covered for 15 minutes. Add flour and cook 15 minutes, frequently stirring to prevent sticking. Add parsley, cream, Velveeta cheese, garlic, salt & pepper. Cook on low heat for 30 minutes. Cook chicken breast and sausage on grill until done, slice. Cook fettucine noodles, according to directions and drain. Mix cream mixture, noodles & grilled chicken and sausage. Pour into 2 large casserole dishes. Bake 15-20 minutes at 350° until heated through. Freezes well. Serves 16-20.

Ann Doggett's Cannelloni

Meat Filling:
- 1 tablespoon olive oil
- 1 tablespoon butter
- ½ cup onion, finely chopped
- 1 teaspoon minced garlic
- 1 10-ounce package frozen chopped spinach, thawed & squeezed dry
- 1½ pounds extra lean ground beef
- 5 tablespoons Parmesan cheese, grated
- 2 tablespoons whipping cream
- 2 eggs, beaten
- ½ teaspoon oregano
- ½ teaspoon salt
- ¼ teaspoon pepper

Sauté onion & garlic in oil & butter until soft. Stir in spinach & cook 3-4 minutes stirring constantly. When all moisture has cooked away, transfer to a large bowl. Brown meat & add to spinach mixture. Add parmesan cheese, whipping cream, eggs, oregano, salt & pepper. Mix well. Can be made ahead.

Tomato Sauce:
- 2 tablespoons olive oil
- 1 cup yellow onions, finely chopped
- 4 cups (2 16-ounce cans) diced Italian plum tomatoes, undrained
- 6 tablespoons tomato paste
- 2 teaspoons dried basil, or fresh
- 2 teaspoons sugar
- 1 teaspoon salt
- 1 teaspoon pepper

Heat oil & sauté onions. Add tomatoes & juice, tomato paste, basil, sugar, salt and pepper. Simmer for 40 minutes and cool slightly. Blend in food processor.

Besciamella:
Melt butter, stir in flour. Add milk and cream all at once, stirring constantly with whisk. When the sauce come to a boil and is smooth, reduce heat. Simmer stirring until thick enough to coat a spoon. Season with salt and white pepper.

- 3 fresh lasagna noodles each cut into 8 equal pieces
- 4 tablespoons Parmesan cheese to put on top after assembly

Assembly Instructions for Cannelloni:
Pour a thin layer of tomato sauce in a shallow baking dish. Fill each piece of lasagna noodle with meat mixture and roll up. Place seam down in baking dish. Pour besciamella over cannelloni and spoon the rest of tomato sauce on top. Sprinkle with parmesan cheese. Bake at 375° for 20-25 minutes. Makes 24 cannelloni.

Note: This recipe freezes well, but freeze before baking. When ready to use, thaw and bake.

Margaret's Rice with Almonds & Currants

4	tablespoons butter	1½	tablespoons fresh marjoram, chopped	
2	tablespoons onion, minced			
2	cups celery, chopped		Fresh ground pepper, to taste	
1	cup Rice, uncooked	1	cup slivered almonds, toasted	
1	teaspoon salt	1½	cups red or golden currants, halved	
1½	cups chicken broth			

Melt butter in a large skillet. Add onion, celery & rice. Cook & stir over medium heat, 3-5 minutes or until rice becomes a pale wheat color. Add salt & chicken broth. Cover. Simmer over low heat 25 minutes or until liquid is absorbed. Remove pan from heat. Stir in marjoram, & season with pepper. Gently stir in almonds & currants until combined. Serve immediately. Serves 6.

Note: Any long grain rice will do, but Texas Basmati is the best. This is especially flavorful, festive rice that is great during the holidays served with lamb, turkey & pork tenderloin. The currants can be substituted with seedless red grapes or golden raisins. I often double or triple the recipe!

Susan's Red Beans & Rice

1	pound package red beans	1	teaspoon Worcestershire
2	ham steaks, chopped in 1" chunks	1	cup celery, chopped
1	package Louis Rich Turkey	1	cup onion, chopped
	Sausage Links, cooked	2	cloves garlic, crushed
2	teaspoons garlic salt	2	bay leaves
1	teaspoon Tabasco		Salt & pepper, to taste

Wash beans well. In a large pot, combine all ingredients except sausage in 1½ cups water. Cook uncovered on low heat about 2½ hours. Add sliced sausage links. Serve over rice.

Margie's Tomato, Basil, & Garlic Sauce

2	cans tomatoes, diced	1	tablespoon garlic, minced
	Fresh basil, chopped		Salt & pepper, to taste
1	tablespoon sugar		

Simmer all together on stove for about 1 hour. Serve over pasta of choice. For heavier dish add chicken or shrimp. Serves 4.

Eggs, Cheese, Bread & Breakfast

Eggs, Cheese, Bread & Breakfast

Preceding Page: The Fauntleroy, Grainger and Cox Families

Top row, left to right: Mitch, Shelley, Ginny, Lara, Parker, John, Robby, Glenda and Rob.

Bottom row, left to right: Mitchell, Parker, Fran and Matthew.

Sandra Tucker's Egg Souffle

8	slices white bread, de-crusted & cubed	½	pound sharp cheese, grated
6	eggs	½	teaspoon salt
3	cups milk	1	teaspoon prepared mustard

Butter a 9x13" Pyrex dish. Cover bottom with cubed bread. Top bread with cheese. Beat eggs, milk, salt & mustard until frothy. Pour over bread. Refrigerate overnight. Bake at 325° for 1 hour & serve hot.

Party Scrambled Eggs

1	dozen eggs	2	tablespoons butter
1	heaping cup cream style cottage cheese		Bacon bits, sausage bits & cheese, optional

Mix ingredients together & scramble in butter in a skillet. Then put scrambled eggs in a greased Pyrex dish & keep warm at 150° until ready to serve. Serves 8-10.

Curried Cheese on Muffins

2	cups grated cheese	½	teaspoon salt
½	cup finely chopped shallots	½	teaspoon (scant) curry powder
½	cup finely chopped ripe olives		English muffins
½	cup mayonnaise		

Mix all ingredients except muffins. Spread on the muffins and place under the broiler until bubbly. Serves 4 or 5, allowing 2 muffins per person.

Mary's Acapulco French Toast

1	loaf regular white bread		*Egg Wash For 2 slices of French Toast:*
1	jar apricot preserves	1	egg
1	cup oil	1	tablespoon vanilla
1	stick butter	1	tablespoon milk

Beat eggwash ingredients until fluffy. Remove crust from bread. Heat 1 stick butter with 1 cup oil until quite hot. Spread apricot preserves thinly on bread then cover with another piece of bread (like a sandwich), slice diagonally. Dip halves into egg wash on both sides. Fry in heated butter and oil until golden on both sides. Drain on paper towels. Sprinkle with cinnamon sugar while hot. Serve with syrup.

Top Secret Pancakes

1¼	cups flour	1	teaspoon baking soda
1½	cups buttermilk	⅓	cup cream of wheat (instant-dry)
1	egg	¼ -½	cup oil
⅓	cup sugar	½	teaspoon salt
1	teaspoon baking powder		

Preheat griddle or skillet to medium. Combine the flour, buttermilk, cream of wheat, egg, sugar, baking powder, baking soda, oil and salt in a large bowl. Mix until smooth (use a mixer if desired). Cook, turning when bubbles appear. Makes 8-12 pancakes.

Shelley's Pimento Cheese

2 cups sharp Cheddar cheese, grated

1 cup Monterey Jack cheese, grated

1 4-ounce jar pimientos, chopped

½ cup mayonnaise

⅓ cup green onions, chopped

Pepper to taste

Combine all ingredients. Better if the mayonnaise is used sparingly. Chill & serve with crackers.

Chubby's Pimento Cheese

1 cup Colby cheese, grated

1 cup sharp Cheddar cheese, grated

½ cup green onions, chopped

1 4-ounce jar pimentos, chopped

Mayonnaise to desired consistency

¼ cup purple onion, chopped

Dash Worcestershire

Combine all ingredients. Makes a wonderful sandwich plain or grilled.

Note: Try on rye bread, sesame rounds, or any crackers.

Aunt Mary's Cheese Souffle

¼ cup butter

¼ cup flour

1 cup milk

1 cup cheese, grated

1 teaspoon salt

½ teaspoon mustard

½ teaspoon paprika

4 eggs, separated

Make a white sauce using butter, flour & milk. Add cheese & seasonings. Cool slightly. Beat egg yolks until thick. Stir into cheese mixture. Fold in stiffly beaten egg whites. Bake in a 1½ quart casserole in a slow oven, 300-325° for 50-60 minutes, or until well browned & firm to the touch. Serve at once. Serves 6.

Old Fashioned Grits

2	cups Quick Grits, not instant	2	cups milk
4	cups water	4	eggs
2	teaspoons salt	1	stick butter or margarine

Cook grits & salt in water over low heat. Boil for 3 minutes. This will become very thick. Warm 1 cup of milk & add to grits. Cover & cook for 5 more minutes. Mix eggs & remainder of milk. Add this to grits. Stirring rapidly, add butter. Pour into a baking dish & bake for about an hour at 350°. You may add 2 cups grated Velveeta, Cheddar or American cheese, if desired.

Douglas' Christmas Birthday Breakfast Cake

1	8-ounce package refrigerated crescent rolls	½	cup granulated sugar
1	8-ounce package cream cheese	¼	cup granulated sugar
1	egg yolk	½	teaspoon cinnamon
¾	teaspon vanilla or almond extract	¼	cup pecans or almonds, chopped (optional)

Soften cream cheese. Beat egg yolk, vanilla & ½ cup sugar into cheese. Put half of crescent rolls in bottom of 8x8" square baking pan. Spread cream cheese mixture over rolls. Top with remainder of rolls. Mix ¼ cup sugar with cinnamon & nuts, and sprinkle over rolls. Bake at 350° for 30 minutes.

Mary Kelly's Irish Bread

2	cups buttermilk	1	teaspoon baking soda
2	cups whole wheat flour	½	cup sugar
1	cup white flour	1	teaspoon salt
2	teaspoons baking powder	1	cup raisins, optional

Mix baking powder & soda into milk. Combine flours, sugar & salt. Add to milk. Add raisins. Grease 2 small 7" bread loaf pans, or a large baking bowl. Bake at 375° for 30-45 minutes.

Dwight Corbin's Monkey Bread

1	cup scalded milk	1	yeast cake
1	cup mashed potatoes	½	cup luke warm water
⅔	cup shortening	2	eggs, well beaten
1	teaspoon salt	5-6	cups flour
⅔	cup granulated sugar	3	sticks butter, melted

Combine scalded milk, potatoes, shortening, salt & sugar. Mix & let cool to lukewarm. Dissolve yeast in water & add to potato mixture. Stir in eggs & add 1½ cups flour. Mix well. Continue adding flour until dough is stiff. Turn out on a floured board & knead very well. Place in greased bowl, brush top with melted butter. Cover top of bowl loosely with wax paper or a dish towel, place in a warm area & let rise for 2 hours. Place in refrigerator. About 1½-2 hours before serving, roll out to ½-inch thick. Cut into 2-inch diamonds. Pull each diamond shape, dip in butter & put in 2 well buttered 2-quart ring molds. Stagger layers of diamonds so they are not directly atop each other. Layer dough evenly in both molds until all diamond cuts are used. Let rise 1 hour, or until it doubles in size. Bake at 400° for 20-25 minutes. This recipe is well worth the trouble.

Bev & Kate's Angel Bisk-Rolls

5	cups flour	1	cup shortening
¼	cup granulated sugar	2	cups buttermilk
1	teaspoon salt	1	package yeast
3	teaspoons baking powder	¼	cup warm water
1	teaspoon baking soda	1	stick butter, melted

Mix dry ingredients. Cut shortening into dry ingredients. Mix yeast in warm water according to package directions. Add mixture. Add buttermilk. Turn out onto floured board & knead to desired consistency. Roll out to ½" thick & cut with biscuit cutter. Dip each one in melted butter & fold in half. Place on cookie sheet. Bake at 400° for 10-15 minutes.

Note: These freeze very well.

Julia's Cinnamon Roll Icing

⅓	cup soft butter (see note)	3	tablespoons cream or whole milk
3	cups powdered sugar		
1	teaspoon vanilla	½	teaspoon almond flavoring

Cream ingredients together. Use only enough cream/milk to make icing spreadable, but not runny. Frost Julia's Cinnamon Rolls while slightly warm & serve!

Note: May substitute half butter & half cream cheese.

Julia's Cinnamon Rolls

½ cup warm water (110-115°)
1 package active dry yeast
½ cup butter
½ cup sugar
2 eggs
1 cup instant mashed potatoes
1 teaspoon salt

1 cup milk, scalded
5-5½ cups flour

Cinnamon Sugar Mixture:
½ cup brown or white sugar
2 teaspoons cinnamon
½ cup raisins (if desired)

Turn oven to warm (you will later place dough in for rising). Soften yeast in warm water. Let stand until needed. In another bowl, cream butter until softened; add sugar gradually, beating well after each time. Add eggs, one at a time, beating well after each addition. Beat mixture until light and fluffy. In a third bowl, mix mashed potatoes, salt and scalded milk together; add gradually to creamed mixture, beating until thoroughly blended. Beat in 1 cup flour. Stir softened yeast and beat into main mixture. Beat enough of the flour (approximately 4 cups) to make soft dough.

Turn dough onto floured surface (using some of the remaining flour) and knead until smooth & satiny (takes approximately 10 minutes). Form dough into ball and put into a greased large bowl. (Crisco is fine). Turn dough to bring greased surface to top. Cover with waxed paper and a towel. Turn oven off & place covered bowl into warm oven. Leave in until dough has doubled (about an hour). Punch down dough (beat until the air is out) and turn it onto a lightly floured surface. Cover and allow to rest 5-10 minutes. Roll out dough into oblong shape. Spread with 2 tablespoons softened butter and sprinkle with cinnamon-sugar mixture & raisins (if desired). Roll up tightly beginning at the wide side. Seal well by pinching edges of roll together. Stretch roll slightly to even (consistent diameter) with no big bulges in middle. Cut roll into 1" slices Place a little apart in greased 13x9" pan or two 9" round pans

Cover & let rise (in warm oven) until double in bulk. (Make sure oven is off.) Should take less than an hour, probably about 45 minutes. Bake until golden brown at 375° for 25-30 minutes. While slightly warm frost with Julia's Cinnamon Roll Icing. Makes 16-20 rolls.

Kate McConns' Banana Bread

3	medium bananas, very ripe	3	eggs
1	teaspoon baking soda	1	teaspoon vanilla
1	stick butter, softened	1	cup pecans, chopped
1	cup granulated sugar	2	cups flour, sifted
1	teaspoon salt		

Mash bananas. Add soda & set aside. With mixer, beat in sugar & salt to softened butter. Add eggs one at a time & cream. Add vanilla, mashed bananas, & nuts. Mix in flour by hand. Grease & flour loaf pan. Pour in batter & bake at 350° about 1 hour.

Bran Muffins

5	cups All Bran Cereal	2½	cups white flour
2½	cups raisins	2	tablespoons baking soda
2	cups boiling water	1	teaspoon salt
½	cup canola oil	2	teaspoons cinnamon
2	cups molasses	¼	teaspoon ground ginger
4	eggs, beaten	½	teaspoon ground cloves
1	quart buttermilk	1	teaspoon baking powder
2½	cups whole wheat flour		Cooking spray

Preheat oven to 350°. Combine All Bran & raisins. Cover with boiling water & let stand for 5 minutes. Add remaining ingredients & blend well. (Too much blending will cause muffins to be tough). Let set at least 2 hours. Spray muffin tins with cooking spray. Fill muffin tins until almost full & bake for 20-25 minutes or until firm.

Note: Batter may be stored in a tightly covered container in the refrigerator for up to 2 months. Baked muffins also freeze well.

Gladys' Cheddar Biscuits

2	cups flour	1½	cups extra Sharp Cheddar
1	tablespoon baking powder		cheese
½	teaspoon salt	1½	cups heavy cream

Sift together flour, baking powder & salt. Add cheese & mix well. Add cream & mix to form dough. Knead dough gently about 6 times on a lightly floured board. Roll & pat dough to ½" thick. Cut with 1" cutter, dip in flour & put on ungreased baking sheet. Bake in preheated oven at 425° for 15 minutes or until golden brown on top. Cool.

Mimi's Hot Water Cornbread

1	cup corn meal	1	teaspoon sugar
¼	cup flour	4-6	tablespoons bacon grease
½	teaspoon salt		

Mix all ingredients & add enough boiling water to create a consistency of cake batter. Drop by tablespoons full into hot grease. Press down with fork or press with table-spoon. Fry until browned evenly.

Cinnamon Rolls

Use Jerry's Ice Box roll dough (see next page, 162). Roll into a sheet ½ inch thick, spread with melted butter or butter substitute. Sprinkle generously with blended sugar/cinnamon mixture (2 tablespoons cinnamon per cup of sugar). Roll and cut cinnamon rolls, place in baking pan. Sprinkle generously again with sugar/cinnamon mixture. Place on well oiled baking sheet, cover with warm, damp cloth until rises to triple in bulk. Bake in hot oven (425°) for approximately 20 minutes. Sprinkle powdered sugar on rolls while still hot.

Jerry's Ice Box Rolls

1	cake dry yeast or 1 cake compressed yeast	6	tablespoons sugar
1	egg, well beaten	2	cups lukewarm water
2	teaspoon salt	3	tablespoons melted shortening
		6½	cups flour

Soften yeast in lukewarm water. If dry yeast is used, combine the sugar, yeast and water and allow to stand in a warm place for 1½ hours. If compressed yeast is used, allow to stand in lukewarm water for 5 minutes. Add salt, egg, sugar (if sugar has not already been added) and shortening. Mix well. Add flour, a little at a time, beating thoroughly after each addition, until dough is stiff enough to knead. Knead on lightly floured board until the dough is smooth and elastic. Cover dough with a warm damp cloth. Set in a moderately warm place and allow to stand 2 hours. Work dough down, cover closely with waxed paper, place in refrigerator overnight. When ready to bake rolls, remove desired portion of dough and let warm to room temperature (approximately 2 hours). Form into rolls, cover and let rise until triple in bulk. Place on well oiled baking sheet and bake in hot oven (450°) for approximately 15 minutes. This dough will keep for 7-10 days in refrigerator, if it is worked down each day to prevent it becoming too light. Keep dough closely covered to prevent a crust from forming.

Mae's 2-4-6 Shortbread

2   ounces granulated sugar
4   ounces butter
6   ounces flour

Cooking spray
Almonds or cherries

Combine sugar & flour. Soften butter & add to dry ingredients. Form a ball of dough, & roll out on a lightly floured board. cut into strips or rounds. Sprinkle lightly with extra sugar. Place almond or cherry on top of each strip & bake on a lightly greased cookie sheet. Bake at 350° for 10-15 minutes.

Jalapeño Cornbread

1   cup cornmeal
½   teaspoon baking powder
¾   teaspoon salt
1   cup buttermilk
2   beaten eggs
½   cup melted butter

1   medium onion, chopped
1   17-ounce can yellow cream style corn
1   cup grated sharp cheese
1   chopped jalapeño

Preheat oven to 350°. Mix all ingredients except cheese and jalapeño, and pour half in a hot greased 9x9" pan. Spread cheese and jalapeño mixture. Pour rest of cornmeal mixture on top. Cook for 45 minutes and cool before serving. Serves 8.

Almeta's Biscuits

5 cups flour
2 cups shortening
½ cup milk

3 teaspoons baking powder
2 teaspoon salt

Mix together 4 cups flour, 1½ cups shortening, salt and baking powder. Mix well. Add milk and mix well again. Melt ½ cup shortening. Let cool. Roll the dough with a rolling pin; fold it over and roll again. Cut the dough into the size biscuit you like, dip in shortening, and bake on a cookie sheet in a 400° oven until brown.

Elizabeth's Artichoke Bread

¼ cup butter or margarine
2-3 cloves garlic, pressed
2 teaspoons sesame seeds
1 14-ounce can artichoke hearts, drained and chopped
1 cup shredded Monterey Jack cheese

1 cup grated Parmesan cheese
½ cup sour cream
1 16-ounce loaf unsliced French bread
½ cup shredded cheddar cheese

Melt butter in a skillet over medium-high heat. Add garlic and sesame seeds; cook, stirring constantly, until lightly browned. Remove from heat. Stir in artichoke hearts and next 3 ingredients. Cover and refrigerate, if desired. If refrigerated, let artichoke mixture stand at room temperature 10 minutes before assembling. Cut bread in half lengthwise. Scoop out center of each half, leaving a 1" shell; set shells aside. Crumble removed pieces of bread, and stir into artichoke mixture. Spoon mixture into shells, and sprinkle with cheddar cheese. Place each half on a baking sheet, and cover with aluminum foil. Bake at 350° for 25 minutes; uncover and bake for 5 minutes or until cheese melts. Cut into slices. Yield: 12 servings.

Lara's English Teatime Scones

2	cups flour, self-rising	¾	cup buttermilk
2	teaspoons baking powder		Raisins, to taste
½	teaspoon nutmeg		Cooking spray
4	tablespoons butter		Strawberry jam
2	tablespoons sugar		Whipping cream
1	large egg		Powdered sugar

Heat oven to 375°. In large bowl, mix all dry ingredients except sugar. Add butter & cut into dry ingredients with a pastry blender until mixture looks like granules. Add raisins & sugar. Put buttermilk in another bowl & lightly whisk in egg yolk. Add egg & buttermilk mixture to flour mixture. Stir until soft dough forms. On lightly floured surface, roll out dough to a 2" thickness. Cut into individual scones with cookie cutter. Place scones close together on a lightly greased cookie sheet.

In a small bowl, whisk the egg white. Brush top of each scone with egg white & sprinkle with granulated sugar. Bake 15-20 minutes, or until golden brown. Cool on a wire rack. To serve, slice each scone in half. Spread with strawberry jam & a tablespoon of whipping cream. Replace top & sprinkle with powdered sugar.

Fried Garlic Bread

1	loaf French bread	½	cup parsley, chopped
1	jar Lawry's Garlic Butter Spread	1	stick margarine or butter Worcestershire, to taste

Slice bread about 1" thick. Melt other ingredients in iron skillet. Mix well & simmer a few minutes. Dip each side of bread into mixture & place on a cookie sheet. Cover with foil until ready to serve. At the last minute, place bread, uncovered in a 400-450° oven until brown on top. Flip over & brown on the other side. A real treat with gumbo or Italian dishes.

Note: For variation with Italian dishes, you can add 1 teaspoon of oregano or basil to butter mixture before dipping for extra flavor!

Beth's Breakfast Casserole

Remove crust from 13 slices of bread

1 pound Owens Sausage, (½ regular, ½ hot)

1 pound Cheddar cheese, grated

1 teaspoon dry mustard, mix into milk

2 cups milk

9 eggs, beaten

¼ teaspoon white pepper

Fry sausage & drain well. Butter 7 slices of bread on both sides and cut into cubes. Place cubes in bottom of large buttered casserole. Mix eggs, milk & pepper well and pour over bread crumbs. Top with grated cheese. Refrigerate overnight. Bake at 350° for 1 hour or until browned completely.

Marilyn's Treasure Cake
Breakfast Cake

1 cup butter

1 cup granulated sugar

2 eggs, whole

2 teaspoons vanilla

Pinch of salt

2 cups cake flour, sifted

1 teaspoon baking powder

1 teaspoon soda

1 cup sour cream

Topping:

½ cup brown sugar

½ cup granulated sugar

1 teaspoon vanilla

1 cup pecans, chopped

To make cake, cream butter, sugar, vanilla, eggs, & salt together. Sift together remainder of dry ingredients. Add ½ of the flour mixture & ½ of the sour cream to the butter mixture. Beat 1 minute. Add remaining flour mixture & sour cream and beat 1 minute. Grease & flour a 9x12x2" pan & spread ½ of the cake batter in pan, reserving the remainder.

Topping: Combine all ingredients. Sprinkle ½ of topping mixture over ½ of the cake batter in pan. Carefully add remaining cake batter and top with remaining topping. Bake in 350° oven for 35-38 minutes.

Pies, Cakes & Frostings

Pies, Cakes & Frostings

Preceding Page: The Glauser, Ayala & Clemens Families

Top row, left to right: Vince, Juan, Gloria, Blakeley, Alicia, Matt & William

Bottom row, left to right: Sterling, Pat, Chandler, Matthew, Ronnie & Harrison.

Alicia's Double French Silk Pie

1	10" cookie pie crust	2	teaspoons vanilla
1	cup butter	4	eggs
1½	cups granulated sugar	2	cups whipping cream or
2	squares unsweetened		Cool Whip
	chocolate, melted		

Cream butter & sugar thoroughly. Add vanilla & chocolate. Add eggs, 1 at a time, beating 5 minutes between each egg. Pour mixture into 10" pie shell. Refrigerate at least 1 hour. Top with whipping cream or Cool Whip to provide fewer calories. Then add additional cookie crumbs left over from pie shell. Serves 8.

Matthew's Cookie Crumb Crust

Crush any kind of cookies, even Oreos. Mix with 1 stick of melted butter until well blended. Press into bottom of pie plate.

Note: Wonderful crust for any cream pie, especially Eagle Brand Lemon.

Chandler's Hot Fudge Pie

2	eggs	¼	cup butter
¼	cup flour	2	ounces unsweetened
1	cup sugar		chocolate
1	teaspoon vanilla		

Sift flour & sugar. Beat eggs. Add flour mixture to eggs. Add vanilla. Melt together in a microwave oven, chocolate & butter. Add to other mixture. Blend well. Pour into buttered pie plate. Bake at 375° for 15-20 minutes. Serve hot.

Note: Top with ice cream or whipped cream.

Easy Peach Cobbler

½	cup butter or margarine		Pinch of salt
1	30-ounce can peaches in syrup	1½	teaspoon baking powder
			Cinnamon, to taste (optional)
1	cup granulated sugar	1	cup milk
¾	cup flour, all purpose		

Melt butter in a 13x9x2" pan. Pour peaches with juice over melted butter. Mix remaining ingredients together until smooth consistency. Pour batter over peaches. Bake at 350° for 1 hour. Crust will rise during the baking.

Note: Fresh peaches are wonderful when in season. Slice 8-12 peaches, cover with sugar & let stand in sugar to create juice.

Lucy's Chocolate Silk Pie & Crust

½	cup butter		*Pie Crust:*
¾	cup granulated sugar	1	cup flour, plain or self-rising
2	eggs	½	cup butter, softened
1	square bitter chocolate	¼	cup chopped pecans
1	teaspoon vanilla	¼	cup powdered sugar
½	pint whipping cream		

Cream butter with sugar. Melt chocolate & blend in. Add vanilla. Add eggs one at a time, beating for 5 minutes after each egg (medium speed with mixer). Turn into cooked pie shell & chill for 1-2 hours before serving. Whip cream & top pie for serving.

Crust: Heat oven to 400°. Mix ingredients with hands to soft dough. Press firmly into bottom & sides (NOT ON RIM) of 9" pie pan. Bake 12-15 minutes or until light brown. Cool.

Note: If you use a foil pie pan, it will not stick.

Patsy Roach's Cherry Pie

1	cup granulated sugar	¼	teaspoon almond extract
¼	cup flour	1 ⅓	tablespoon butter
¼	teaspoon cinnamon		Pie Crust Recipe below
1	can red, sour cherries, pitted		

In saucepan, combine sugar, flour, cinnamon & undrained cherries. Cook over medium heat, stirring constantly until mixture thickens & boils (about 7 minutes). Remove from heat. Stir in extract. Pour into 9" pastry lined pan. Dot with butter. Roll out top crust & cup into ½-¾" strips weaving them into a lattice pattern over cherries. Blend edges into bottom crust & crimp entire outer edge. Bake at 425° for 30-35 minutes until nicely browned & juice bubbles through openings in crust.

Pie Crust:

3	cups flour	1	cup Crisco
1½	teaspoon salt	4	tablespoons Crisco
		6	tablespoons COLD water

Measure flour into bowl & mix salt through it. With pastry blender or 2 knives, cut in shortening until the particles are size of giant peas. Sprinkle with water, a tablespoon at a time, mixing lightly with a fork until all flour is moist. Gather dough together with fingers so it cleans the bowl. Press firmly into a ball. Cut ball in half & press each into another firm ball. Roll out on a lightly floured pastry cloth to ⅛" thickness. Roll lightly, being careful not to add extra flour as that makes pastry tough. Keep pastry circular & roll it at least 1" larger than an inverted pie pan to line pan. Allow for depth & folding under the edges before crimping.

Sue Kourim's Chocolate Cake

Cake:

1	box yellow cake mix (without pudding)
1	4-ounce box instant chocolate fudge pudding
1	4-ounce box French vanilla pudding
4	eggs
1¼	cups water
⅓	cup oil
1	6-ounce bag semi-sweet chocolate chips
1	6-ounce bag milk-chocolate chips

Chocolate Glaze:

1	14-ounce can Eagle Brand Sweetened Condensed Milk
1	12-ounce pack semi-sweet chocolate chips
1½	teaspoons vanilla

Plain Glaze:

½	cup powdered sugar
½	teaspoon vanilla or almond extract
1½	tablespoons cream or milk

Combine cake mix, pudding mix, eggs, water & oil. Stir in chocolate chips. Pour in lightly greased & floured bundt pan. Bake at 350° for 1 hour.

Chocolate Glaze: Heat milk. Add chips, stirring until completely melted. Add vanilla. Pour over warm cake.

Plain Glaze: Mix well until smooth. Spread over warm cake.

Sour Cream Chocolate Cake

2   cups all purpose flour,
     unsifted
2   cups sugar
1   cup water
¾   cup sour cream
¼   cup butter
1¼   teaspoons baking soda

1   teaspoon salt
1   teaspoon vanilla extract
½   teaspoon baking powder
2   eggs
4   ounces unsweetened baking
     chocolate, melted
4   cups powdered sugar
1   cup sour cream
2   teaspoons vanilla extract

Frosting:
½   cup butter
4   ounces unsweetened baking
     chocolate

Preheat oven to 350 dgerees. Measure all ingredients into large bowl & beat for about 30 seconds. Then beat at high speed for 3 minutes. Pour into greased & floured cake pans (2- 9" or 3-8"). Bake for 20-25 minutes. Remove from the oven & cool on a rack.

Frosting: In the top of a double boiler, melt butter & chocolate over barely simmering water. Remove from heat & cool. Add powdered sugar, then blend in sour cream & vanilla. Beat until smooth.

Note: This rich chocolate cake freezes beautifully & looks as good as it tastes!

Lillian Jackson's Caramel Cake

2	sticks butter		*Frosting:*	
2	cups granulated sugar		2	sticks butter
4	eggs		2	cups granulated sugar
3	cups flour		2	cups Half & Half
2	teaspoons baking powder		2	teaspoons vanilla
1	cup milk			
1	tablespoon vanilla			

Cream butter, sugar & eggs. Add milk & vanilla. Add flour & baking powder. Mix well. Pour into 3 layer pans or 1, 9x12" baking pan. Bake at 375° for 30-35 minutes. Cool & ice.

Frosting: Combine ingredients & cook over medium heat about 30 minutes or until thick enough to pour over cake. Pour over cake or spead between layers.

Thomas' Cheesecake

1½	cups graham cracker crumbs		*Frosting:*	
1	cup pecans, finely chopped		1½	pints sour cream
½	cup unsalted butter		½	cup granulated sugar
1½	pounds cream cheese		1	tablespoon lemon juice (or vanilla)
4	eggs			
1	tablespoon lemon juice			

Combine crumbs, pecans & melted butter to make crust. Press into a 13x9x2" spring-form pan. Soften cream cheese & add eggs, sugar, lemon & beat until creamy. Pour over crust. Bake 20-25 minutes at 350°.

Frosting: Combine sour cream, sugar & lemon juice with mixer until smooth. Spread over top of hot cheesecake. Let rest until cooled. Refrigerate.

Note: Vanilla can be substituted for the lemon juice.

Gladys' Lemon Tea Cakes

1¼	cup flour, sifted	1	teaspoon vanilla
⅔	cup sugar	2	teaspoons lemon rind, finely grated
½	teaspoon baking powder		
¼	teaspoon salt	¾	cup butter, melted & cooled
3	eggs		Powdered sugar for top

Sift together flour, baking powder & salt. Beat eggs until light. Add vanilla. Gradually beat in sugar & continue beating until volume has increased to about 4 times the original size. Fold in lemon rind. Gradually fold into flour mixture. Then stir in butter. Brush tiny muffin cups with butter. Spoon about 1 tablespoon of batter into each cup filling about ¾ full. Bake at 350° for 12-15 minutes or until golden brown. Remove cakes to cooling rack and sift powdered sugar on top of each. Makes 3 dozen.

Aunt Mary's Devil's Food Cake

2	cups sugar	1	teaspoon allspice
1	cup butter	1	teaspoon nutmeg
4	eggs		
½	cup cocoa		*Icing:*
½	cup hot water	3	cups sifted powdered sugar
1	teaspoon baking soda	3	teaspoons cocoa, sifted
½	cup buttermilk	3	teaspoons vanilla
2½	cups flour, more as needed	3	tablespoons liquid coffee
1	teaspoon cinnamon	1	cup butter

Cream sugar & butter. Add beaten eggs, buttermilk & soda. Combine cocoa & hot water and add to mixture. Stir all together and add flour & spices. Pour in 9x11" pan & bake at 350° for 30 minutes. Check with toothpick to be sure it is done.
Icing: Mix all together & spread over cooled cake.

Mary's Applesauce Cake

Mix:
- 2   cups sugar
- ½   cup butter

Add:
- 2   eggs, well beaten
- 3   tablespoons white vinegar
- 1½   cups stewed apples or apple sauce or juice of spiced peaches

Mix:
- 2½   cups flour
- 2   teaspoons baking soda
- ¾   teaspoon allspice
- ½   teaspoon ground cloves
- 3   teaspoons baking powder

Add:
- 1   teaspoons vanilla
- 1½   cups raisins
- 1   cup pecans, chopped

Bake in 300-325° oven for 2 hours.

Phillis Cake

Sift together:
- 2   cups flour
- 2   cups sugar

Bring to a boil:
- 1   cup water
- 4   tablespoons cocoa
- 2   sticks butter

Pour this over flour and sugar mixture.

Add:
- ½   cup buttermilk
- 2   eggs, beaten
- 1   teaspoon vanilla

Blend by hand & add:
- 1   cup pecans

Bake at 400° for 20 minutes.

Icing:
- 1   stick butter
- 1   tablespoon milk
- 4   tablespoons cocoa
- 1   box powdered sugar
- 1   teaspoon vanilla
- 1   teaspoon cinnamon

Melt butter & mix all ingredients together. Spread over cooled cake.

Aunt Mary's 5-Minute Jello Cake

1	box yellow cake mix*		*Glaze:*
⅔	cup apricot nectar	1	cup powdered sugar
⅔	cup oil	4	tablespoons melted butter
4	eggs	2	tablespoons fresh lemon juice
½	teaspoon lemon extract		
½	teaspoon butter flavoring	* 1	box lemon jello
	Zest of 1 lemon		

Beat all ingredients at high speed for 5 minutes. Pour into floured tube pan. Bake at 350° for 50 minutes. Cool for 10-20 minutes and glaze.

Old Fashioned Tea Cakes

1	cup butter	2	teaspoons baking powder
2	cups sugar	1	teaspoon vanilla
4	eggs	½	teaspoon nutmeg, optional
4	cups flour		

Cream butter & sugar. Add eggs. Mix baking powder with flour. Add flour mixture gradually to butter mixture. Add vanilla & nutmeg. Chill. When dough is firm roll out on floured paper. Cut and bake at 350° until lightly brown, about 8-10 minutes. Makes 6 dozen.

Aunt Mary's Ginger Apple Crisp

3   pounds baking apples,
      peeled, cored & sliced

2   tablespoons fresh lemon juice

1   tablespoon cornstarch

⅓   cup sugar

¼   teaspoon ground ginger

⅛   teaspoon nutmeg, freshly
      grated

½   cup crystalized ginger,
      chopped

1   cup flour

½   cup brown sugar, firmly
      packed

      Pinch of salt

6   tablespoons unsalted butter,
      cut into pieces

⅓   cup walnuts, chopped

Preheat oven to 400°. In large bowl toss apple slices with lemon juice. In another bowl, stir cornstarch, sugar, ginger, nutmeg, and ginger. Add to apples and coat evenly. Transfer to a 1½ quart pie dish, heaping apples up in the center. In a bowl mix together the flour, brown sugar & salt. Drop in the butter & blend with fingers until crumbly. Add walnuts & toss and stir to combine. Sprinkle evenly over apples.

Bake until top is brown & apples are tender, about 45-50 minutes. Remove from oven & serve warm with favorite ice cream or just plain.

Luc's Coconut Cake

1½	cups sugar	***Filling & Frosting:***	
1½	cups milk	1¼	cups sugar
1	teaspoon vanilla	½	cup milk
2	eggs, separated	½	cup cream
⅔	cup butter		
3	teaspoons baking powder		
2	cups flour		

Mix dry ingredients & add to rest of ingredients. Bake in 2 cake pans at 375° for 20-25 minutes or until toothpick comes out clean.

Filling & Frosting: Bring mixture to a boil & boil very slowly for about 15 minutes. Add enough freshly grated coconut to make spreadable, 1 cup or more.

Bobby's Pineapple-Coconut Pound Cake

1	cup butter, softened	***Icing:***	
2	cups sugar	1	large can crushed pineapple
3	cups flour, sifted	3	tablespoons sugar
4	eggs, beaten	1	tablespoon flour
3	teaspoons baking powder	1	teaspoon vanilla
1	cup milk	1	cup moist coconut
1½	teaspoons vanilla		
¼	teaspoon salt		

Mix sugar, butter & add eggs. Add flour and remainder of ingredients. Mix well & pour into bundt cake pan. Bake at 350° for about 30 minutes.

Icing: Heat pineapple, sugar & flour. Cook for 8 minutes or until thick. Add vanilla. Pour over cooled cake & sprinkle with coconut.

Mary's Lemon Crumble

Filling:

¼	cup lemon juice
	Zest from 1 lemon
2	eggs
1	cup sugar
1	teaspoon cornstarch
1	tablespoon flour
1	tablespoon butter
1	teaspoon vanilla

Cook in double boiler until thickens. Cool. Add vanilla.

Mix:

1¾	cups Ritz Crackers, crumbled
½	cup sugar
¾	cup flour
¾	cup butter
½	cup coconut, toasted
1	teaspoon baking powder

Layer in baking dish, crackers, filling, crackers. Bake at 350° for 30 minutes.

Bin's Buttermilk Chess Pie

1	9" pie shell, uncooked & pierced with fork

Rub inside shell:

1	tablespoon flour
1	tablespoon sugar

Bake 10 minutes. Cool.

Filling:

2	tablespoons flour
1½	cups sugar
1	stick butter

3	eggs, beaten
	Pinch salt
½	cup buttermilk
	Juice of 1-2 lemons
½	teaspoon vanilla

Blend flour, sugar. Melt butter slowly & add eggs. Add flour & sugar mixture. Add remaining ingredients. Pour into cooled pie shell & bake at 300° for 45 minutes.

Light Lemon Icebox Pie

1	teaspoon unflavored gelatin		¼	teaspoon cream of tartar
1	tablespoon cold water		⅛	teaspoon salt
½	cup fresh lemon juice		⅓	cup sugar
2	egg yolks			Lemon slices, optional
1	14-ounce can fat-free sweetened condensed milk		1	Graham cracker crust
3	egg whites at room temperature			

Preheat oven to 325°. Sprinkle gelatin over cold water and set aside. Cook lemon juice and egg yolks in small pan for 10 minutes, stirring constantly. Add gelatin and cook one minute. Place mixture (in pot) in large ice-filled bowl and stir for 3 minutes (do not allow it to set). Gradually add milk. Spoon into graham cracker crust. Beat egg whites, cream of tartar and salt on high until peaks form. Add sugar gradually. Spread over filling. Bake at 325° for 25 minutes. Cool 1 hour on wire rack and chill for 3 hours before serving. Serves 8.

Graham Cracker Crust:

			1	egg white
			1½	cups graham cracker crumbs
2	tablespoons sugar		1	teaspoon cinnamon
1	tablespoon chilled margarine			Cooking spray

Heat oven to 350°. Combine first 3 ingredients & blend on medium mixer speed. Add crumbs & cinnamon & toss with fork. Press into a 9" pie plate, coated with cooking spray. Cook 20 minutes. Let cool & add your favorite pie ingredients.

Pear Tarte

4-5   pears, firm & ripe

2   pie crusts

12   ounces caramel ice cream topping

¼   cup orange liquor

2   tablespoons lemon juice

1   12-ounce can sweetened condensed milk

Orange peel, to taste

Lay out pie crusts & cut into 1" strips. Wrap around pears. To get dough to stick where it overlaps, moisten with water. Cook at 350° for 1 hour or until golden brown. In double-boiler, combine caramel sauce and sweetened condensed milk. Blend until smooth (bring to a boil and reduce heat). Add lemon and liquor and peel.

Note: To serve, pour sauce and set pears in dish. Garnish with mint.

Almeta's Plum Cobbler

2   pounds plums, seeded and cut in fourths

1   cup sugar

½   stick butter

½   teaspoon nutmeg

½   teaspoon cinnamon

1   teaspoon vanilla

Line a deep Pyrex bowl with crust. Put plums, sugar, butter, spices and vanilla in it. Put crust on top. Bake at 350° oven until brown.

Topping:

Philadelphia cream cheese

Cream

Soften cream cheese with cream until desired consistency.

Plum Cobbler Crust:

2   cups flour

1   cup shortening

1   teaspoon baking powder

¼   teaspoon salt

⅓   cup ice water

Mix dry ingredients; then add ice in water. Divide dough in half and roll out. Mold one piece in bottom of Pyrex bowl, add filling and then top crust. Crimp edges of top crust and pierce holes in it with a fork.

Mrs. Brazelton's Lemon Cake

Sponge Cake:

12	egg yolks
2	cups sugar
1	cup boiling water
3	cups sifted cake flour
4	tablespoons baking powder
1	teaspoon salt
1	teaspoon vanilla
½	teaspoon lemon extract

Lemon Jelly Filling:

Juice & rind of 2 lemons

1	cup sugar
2	eggs
2	tablespoons flour
1	tablespoons melted butter

White Icing:

2	egg whites
1	cup white corn syrup
4	tablespoon sugar
½	teaspoon almond extract
½	teaspoon vanilla
¼	teaspoon salt

Sponge Cake: Beat egg yolks until light colored. Gradually add 2 cups sugar while beating. Pour in 1 cup boiling water and continue beating until volume doubles. Sift flour, baking powder and salt. Blend into above mixture a spoon at a time on low mixture speed. Add vanilla and lemon extract. Pour in 11x16" greased & floured pan. Bake at 375° about 40 minutes.

Invert to cool. When cool, split lengthwise in 2 layers. Fill and cover with lemon jelly filling and ice with whipped cream or white icing.

Lemon Jelly Filling: Beat egg yolks. Gradually add sugar. Beat egg whites. Add lemon juice and rind. Add 1 cup boiling water. Stir flour into ½ cup cold water and add. Beat in 1 tablespoon butter. Combine with egg yolk mixture.

White Icing: Beat egg whites & salt to form peaks. In a sauce pan, mix syrup & sugar until sugar is dissolved & mixture boils. Pour syrup slowly over beaten egg whites. When mixture is good consistency for spreading add vanilla & almond extract.

Marion's Blackberry Cobbler

2½	large packages blackberries, frozen	¾	stick butter
1½	cups sugar	¼	teaspoon salt
3	tablespoons flour	2	15-ounce packages Pillsbury Pie Crust (found in dairy counter)
2	tablespoons lemon juice		
1½	teaspoons apple pie spice		

Let pie crust stand at room temperature for 15 minutes. Press out fold lines with fingers. If crust separates, wet fingers & crimp together to seal. Butter a 13½x9x2½" Pyrex dish and cover with raw crust. Mix berries, sugar, flour and spices. Add to the lined dish. Sprinkle top of berry mixture with lemon juice and dollops of butter. Cover with the remaining crust. Cut a design in top crust & sprinkle with sugar. Bake 40-45 minutes in 425° oven.

Hattie's Pecan Pie

1	9" pie crust, uncooked	¼	teaspoon salt
1	cup sugar	3	eggs
1	stick butter, softened	1	cup pecans, chopped
1	cup light corn syrup		

Cream sugar & butter together until smooth. Add syrup, salt & beat well. Beat in eggs, 1 at a time. Add pecans. Pour into pie shell & bake at 350° for about 1 hour & 10 minutes, or until knife comes out clean when inserted in middle of pie. Cool & serve plain or with whipped cream or vanilla ice cream.

Kiki's Baked Alaska

Place a layer of any baked white or yellow cake on an oven-proof china or silver-plated tray (don't use sterling silver). If you are fond of the flavor of rum or brandy, sprinkle the cake generously with one or both. Add fine layer of granulated sugar. Cover with quart of vanilla ice cream in very thick layer. Leave a ½" border around outside of cake free of ice cream. Beat 4 egg whites until stiff & fold in ¾ cup of powdered sugar. Cover cake & ice cream with meringue. Cover, seal completely & pile meringue high. Brown quickly in a 450° oven. Remove & pour 1 ounce of brandy on top. Light & serve at once.

Note: Any flavor of ice cream can be used. Another more elaborate version is to thicken black cherries with cornstarch. Place mixture on tray, add brandy & then light. Fresh, sugared strawberries can also be used instead of cherries.

Lara's Tequila Lime Pie

½	cup butter		⅓	cup lime juice, concentrated
1¼	cups pretzels, finely crushed		2-4	tablespoons tequila
¼	cup granulated sugar		1	cup whipping cream, whipped
1	14-ounce can sweetened condensed milk			

Melt butter & stir in pretzels & sugar. Mix well & press into a 9" baking dish. Place dish in refrigerator for 1 hour. In large bowl, combine condensed milk, lime juice & tequila. Mix well. Fold in whipped cream. Pour into prepared crust. Chill until firm. Garnish with fresh mint leaves & lime slices.

Baby Christiana Cake

1	cup pecans, chopped	½	cup cold water
1	18-ounce yellow cake mix with Jello	⅓	cup vegetable oil
3	eggs	½	cup Bacardi rum, light or dark

Preheat oven to 325°. Grease & flour bundt pan. Sprinkle nuts over bottom. Combine all cake ingredients together. Pour over nuts. Bake 1 hour. Invert on serving place & prick top. Spoon glaze over top & let cake absorb it. Either the Christiana Glaze or Eggnog Glaze are delicious. Try them both.

Christiana's Glaze

¼	pound butter	½	cup Bacardi rum, light or dark
¼	cup water		
1	cup granulated sugar		

Melt butter in sauce pan. Stir in water & sugar. Boil 5 minutes, stirring constantly. Remove from heat & stir in rum.

Eggnog Glaze

1	cup powdered sugar, sifted	1	tablespoon corn syrup, light
1	tablespoon dairy egg nog	1	teaspoon rum, light

Combine sugar, syrup & rum in a small bowl. Add eggnog one teaspoon at a time until you attain the right consistency for glazing the cake.

J J's Palm Beach Pie

1	cup shortbread cookies, crushed	10	Macadamia nuts, in half
¼	cup granulated sugar	4	egg yolks
½	cup Macadamia nuts, chopped	1	3-ounce package cream cheese
5	tablespoons butter, melted	½	cup Key lime juice
1	14-ounce can Eagle Brand sweetened condensed milk	1	cup heavy cream
		¼	cup granulated sugar

Mix cookies, ¼ cup sugar, chopped Macadamia nuts & butter. Press into a 9" pie plate. Put in freezer. Combine egg yolks & milk. Mix cream cheese into milk & egg. Add lime juice a teaspoon at a time. Pour into chilled pie crust & refrigerate for 12-24 hours. When serving, top with whipping cream that has been whipped with another ¼ cup of sugar added to it. Decorate with Macadamia nut halves.

Mimi's 7-Minute Frostings

2	egg whites, unbeaten	1½	teaspoons light corn syrup
1½	cups sugar	1	teaspoon vanilla, white is
5	tablespoons cold water		preferred

Put egg whites, sugar, water and corn syrup in upper part of double boiler. Beat with egg beater until thoroughly mixed. Place over rapidly boiling water, beat constantly with beater and cook for 7 minutes or until frosting will stand in peaks. Remove from fire, add vanilla and beat until thick enough to spread. Covers 2, 9" layers.

Chocolate: Fold 3 squares Baker's Unsweetened Chocolate, melted into 7-Minute Frosting. (Do not beat mixture.) Cool and spread on cake.

Coconut: Add ½ cup Baker's Coconut (Southern Style) to 7-Minute Frosting. Sprinkle ½ cup coconut over cake before frosting becomes firm.

Marshmallow: Add 1 cup marshmallows, quartered, to 7-Minute Frosting before spreading on cake.

Beth's Flag Cake

2	16-ounce packages pound cake mix	⅓	cup confectioner sugar
½	cup milk	1½	teaspoon vanilla extract
4	large eggs	½	pint blueberries
3	cups heavy cream	1	pint raspberries

Whip cream & refrigerate while cake is cooking so cream will set. Take out 3 cups to spread & keep the remaining whipped cream refrigerated while spreading & covering cake. Preheat oven to 350°. Grease & flour 13x9" baking pan. In large bowl mix at low speed both boxes of cake mix and eggs until blended, at medium speed for 4 minutes. Pour into pan & bake 45-50 minutes until toothpick comes out clean. Cool on wire rack 15 minutes. Loosen edges and invert onto rack. Cool completely. When cake is cool, in large bowl beat whipping cream on medium speed, adding sugar and vanilla until stiff peaks form. Place cake on large platter (tray). Spread 3 cups of whipped cream on top & sides. Arrange blueberries & raspberries on top to resemble American Flag. (Blueberries 9 rows total: 5 rows of 6; 4 rows of 5. Raspberries 7 rows total: 4 short; 3 long). Leave space between each row of raspberries for extra whipped cream. Spoon remaining mixture of cream into decorating bag with medium size star tube. Pipe lines between raspberries. Then pipe decorative border around edge of cake. Refrigerate cake until ready to serve.

Gladys' Vanilla Wafer Cake

2	sticks butter, softened	1	cup pecans, chopped
2	cups sugar	½	cup milk
12	ounce box vanilla wafers, crushed	6	eggs

Cream butter and sugar. Add the other ingredients. Bake at 350° for 1 hour and 15 minutes in a bundt or tube pan.

Scottie's Delicious Pumpkin Pie

1	envelope gelatin	½	cup milk
¼	cup cold water	½	teaspoon salt
2	eggs, separated	½	teaspoon nutmeg
1½	cups canned pumpkin	½	teaspoon cinnamon
½	cup brown sugar	¼	cup sugar

Mix 1½ pints whipped cream & 3 tablespoons of sugar. Soften gelatine in ¼ cup hot water. Combine egg yolks, brown sugar, pumpkin, milk, salt, nutmeg & cinnamon in top of double boiler. Cook for 10 minutes. Remove from heat, stir in gelatin & cool. Beat egg whites until foamy; add sugar gradually. Fold into cool pumpkin mixture. Bake in pre-cooked pie shell. Top with whipped cream.

Isla McConn's Chocolate Cake

1	box golden butter cake mix	4	eggs
1	4-ounce box instant chocolate pudding mix	1	teaspoon vanilla
1	cup sour cream	1	12-ounce bag chocolate chips, sweet or semi-sweet
1	cup vegetable oil		

Mix all ingredients. Pour into very lightly greased bundt pan. Bake in preheated 350° oven for 1 hour.

Puddings, Frozen Desserts & Toppings

Puddings, Frozen Desserts & Toppings

Preceding Page: The Reckling Family

Top row, left to right: Isla holding John Jr., Stephen Jr., Douglas, Matthew & John Luke.

Middle row, left to right: Randa, Kate, Thomas V, Mark, Bryant & Kelsey.

Bottom row, left to right: Sterling (holding Christiana), Lauren, Mary Kelly, Hunter, Adelaide, Rienzi (holding Emmy), Betsy & Thomas Kelly.

Inset: Anna

Eileen's *Apricot Whip*

2 packages apricot Jello (do not add water)

1 large container cottage cheese, cream style

Cool Whip (use just enough to make mixture light apricot color)

Combine ingredients and chill. May be served as a salad as well as a dessert.

Floating Island

1 quart milk

4 eggs

4 teaspoons sugar

2 tablespoons cornstarch

½ teaspoon salt

1 teaspoon vanilla

Heat milk in double boiler. Beat egg yolks until light. Add sugar, cornstarch which has been mixed in a little cold water, and salt. Add this gradually to the hot milk, stirring well. Cook for 5 minutes. Add vanilla. Beat egg whites until stiff, adding a little bit of the sugar. Heap mounds of meringue on top of custard and run under the broiler quickly to brown them, if desired. Serves 8.

Almeta's Lemon Mousse

1 cup sugar

½ cup water

8 egg yolks

1½ pints whipping cream

1 cup lemon juice

2 envelopes plain gelatin dissolved in a little cold water.

Mix sugar, water and egg yolks in double boiler. Cook until it begins to thicken. Add gelatin and keep cooking until this is well mixed. Add lemon juice and cook 1 minute more. Let cool. Whip cream and fold into lemon mixture. Pour into a tube cake pan well-greased with butter and put in refrigerator until firm. To unmold, run knife around edges. Do not put in hot water. This is delicious served with cracked lemon drops on it, or topped with strawberries or raspberries. Serves 10-12.

Thomas & Walt's Lemon Bisque

1	13-ounce can Carnation milk	⅓	cup honey
1	package lemon Jello	⅛	teaspoon salt
1¼	cup boiling water	3	tablespoons lemon juice, plus
2½	cups vanilla wafer crumbs		grated rind

Dissolve Jello in water. Add honey, lemon juice and rind until slightly thick. Whip can of milk and fold in. Line pyrex casserole with vanilla wafer crumbs, saving some for the top. Then add Jello mixture and sprinkle with remaining crumbs. Refrigerate. Serves 12.

Bread Pudding with Whiskey Sauce

Bread Pudding:

1	loaf French bread (day old bread is best)
1	cup brown sugar
4	eggs, beaten
½	cup raisins
½	cup apples, peeled & chopped
2-3	tablespoons cinnamon
1	teaspoon nutmeg
1	stick butter
1	cup granulated sugar
¼	cup coconut, shredded
2	teaspoons vanilla

Whiskey Sauce:

1	stick butter
1	cup granulated sugar
¼	cup whiskey
1	teaspoon vanilla
3	tablespoons heavy cream

Bread Pudding: Tear bread into pieces. Beat eggs & combine with other ingredients. Pour over bread, mix well with fork or hands, & pour into a buttered pan. Cook at 350° for 1 hour, or until toothpick comes out clean.

Whiskey Sauce: Melt butter over medium heat. When melted, add sugar & vanilla. Stir over medium heat until bubbly. Add whiskey & remove from heat. Continue to stir while adding cream. Pour over each individual serving.

Note: Pineapple can be exchanged for the apples in the bread pudding recipe for variety.

Bread Pudding with Whiskey Sauce

2	cups milk		*Whiskey Sauce:*	
2	cups coarse bread crumbs, 1-2"	½	cup butter	
¼	cup butter, melted	1	cup sugar	
¼	teaspoon salt	1	egg, beaten	
1	teaspoon ground cinnamon	½	cup whiskey	
½	cup sugar			
2	eggs, slightly beaten			
½	cup seedless raisins			

Scald milk & pour over bread crumbs. Cool & add remaining ingredients, mixing well. Pour into a 1½ quart casserole dish. Bake at 350° for 1 hour or until a silver knife inserted into pudding comes out clean.

Whiskey Sauce: Heat butter & sugar in heavy saucepan, stirring until mixture is very hot & sugar is dissolved. Add egg quickly & heat until smooth. Cool & add whiskey. Serve hot or cold over pudding. Serves 6.

Katie's Butterscotch Sauce

1	egg, well beaten	½	cup corn syrup, light
¼	cup water	¼	cup butter, melted
⅔	cup brown sugar		

Combine egg & water. Add other ingredients & cook in double boiler until thick. Stir frequently while cooking. Pour into jar. Refrigerate.

Note: Sauce is good hot or cold over ice cream.

Dwight's Chocolate Ice Cream

1	6-ounce package semi-sweet chocolate pieces		3	egg yolks
¼	cup granulated sugar		1½	cup heavy cream
⅓	cup water		1	teaspoon vanilla

In small saucepan combine sugar & water. Bring to boil & continue cooking for 3 minutes. Put chocolate chips in blender. Add hot syrup. Cover & blend at high speed for 20 seconds until sauce is smooth. Add 3 egg yolks. Stir to combine, then blend for 10 seconds more. Fold chocolate mixture into cream which has been whipped. Spoon into refrigerator tray (or glass bowl). Cover with waxed paper & freeze for 3 hours. Makes 1 quart.

Note: Mixture will not form ice crystals & doesn't need stirring.

Blakeley's Banana Pudding

1	5-ounce package instant vanilla pudding		2-3	bananas, sliced
3	cups milk		1	box Girl Scout Cinnamon Cookies
1	8-ounce package Cool Whip			
1	can Eagle Brand Sweetened Condensed Milk			

Beat pudding & milk according to package. Fold in Cool Whip & sweetened condensed milk. Crush cookies. Layer cookies, bananas, & pudding until everything is used, ending with the pudding.

Lemon Fruit Ice Box Dessert

½	cup butter		3	egg whites, whipped
1	cup powdered sugar		3	dozen vanilla wafers
3	egg yolks, beaten		½	cup pecans, chopped
¼	cup lemon juice, fresh squeezed		½	pint whipping cream
¼	cup crushed pineapple, drained		¼	teaspoon grated lemon rind

Cream butter & sugar. Add egg yolks & beat 2 minutes. Add juice, rind & pineapple. Fold in whipped egg whites. Line bottom and sides of loaf dish with wafers. Add an inch layer of fruit mixture, cover with wafers, add more fruit & wafers. Use all the ingredients ending with a top layer of wafers. Chill 12 hours or longer. Unmold and sprinkle with nuts & cover with whipped cream. Cut into slices to serve.

Alice Ellington's Lemon Pudding

2	eggs, separated		¼	cup fresh lemon juice
¼	cup flour			Zest of 1 lemon, optional
1	cup sugar			
1	cup milk			

Mix flour & sugar. Add milk & stir well. Add egg yolks that have been well beaten. Add lemon juice. Fold in beaten egg whites. Bake in casserole that is set in shallow pan of water in a low oven of 300-325° for 40-60 minutes.

Baby Anna's Rollin' Good Ice Cream

1	cup Half & Half	1	12-ounce clean coffee can & lid
1	cup heavy cream		
½	cup granulated sugar	1	39-ounce clean coffee can & lid
1	teaspoon vanilla (or almond) extract		
		2	cups rock salt

Mix cream, Half & Half, sugar, and flavoring. Pour mixture into the small coffee can. Be sure the lid is tight. Place the can containing mixture into the large coffee can. Fill with ice & half the rock salt. Let the children roll the can around, back & forth for about 10 minutes. Remove the lid & drain the water. Carefully open small can & stir the mixture. Replace the lid. Add more ice & salt to large can, & roll around for 10 more minutes. Open carefully & spoon out.

Note: You may add sliced fruit (¾ cup), nuts or candy for variety.

Judy Lee's Fresh Strawberry Ice Cream

4	pints fresh strawberries	4	cups whipping cream
	Juice of 2 lemons	2	cups Half & Half cream
3¼	cups sugar		

Wash and destem strawberries. Chop them in blender. Add lemon juice, sugar and chill. Add whipping cream, and half and half. Mix thoroughly and freeze in an ice cream freezer.

Mamo's Apricot Soufflé

6	egg whites	1	cup apricots, stewed
1	teaspoon baking powder	½	pint whipping cream
1	cup granulated sugar	¼	cup sugar
½	tablespoon lemon juice	1	teaspoon vanilla

Stew package of dry apricots in water according to directions. Drain & run through a sieve with all juice taken out. Pack 1 cup of apricot pulp tightly with lemon juice added. Pack tightly into cup. Beat eggs dry & slowly add 1 cup sugar, beating constantly. Add apricots by the spoonful. Add baking powder. Grease a souffle dish & pour in mixture. Bake at 350° for 40 minutes, turning dish twice. Beat whipping cream until it forms peaks & add sugar & vanilla. Serve mixture atop soufflé.

Note: For a different topping than the whipped cream, try Almeta's Cerise Sauce.

Almeta's Cerise Sauce

1½	cups powdered sugar	1	egg white, unbeaten
	Pinch salt	2	tablespoons butter
2	egg yolks	1	teaspoon vanilla

Cream butter, sugar, salt & eggs. When quite smooth, add vanilla. Good on souffles, pies or puddings. Recipe may also be frozen.

Note: A touch of bourbon is good for flavoring, & you can substitute maraschino cherry juice for vanilla for a different approach. Just as good if not better.

Margaret Fraser's Banana Pudding

1½	cups sugar	3	tablespoons butter, melted
6	tablespoons flour	1	teaspoon vanilla
4	eggs, separated	1	box vanilla wafers
3	cups milk	3	bananas, sliced

Mix sugar and flour in one bowl. In second bowl, beat egg yolks until smooth and light yellow. Add milk gradually. Pour both together and add butter, blending thoroughly. Cook over medium heat stirring constantly until thickened. Add vanilla and cool. In a 9x13" baking dish, layer wafers, bananas and pudding. Top with meringue.

Meringue:
- 4 egg whites
- 8 tablespoons sugar
- 1 teaspoon vanilla

Beat egg whites until stiff. Slowly beat in sugar. Fold in vanilla. Cover cooled pudding and bake in 350° oven until golden brown.

Carol's Fantastic Fudge Pudding

4	cups sugar	2	cups butter, melted
1	cup all purpose flour	4	teaspoons vanilla
1	cup cocoa	2	cups pecans, chopped
8	large eggs		

Preheat oven 300°. Sift together sugar, flour & cocoa. Beat eggs in large bowl. Add dry ingredients, butter & vanilla. Mix well, stir in pecans and pour into 3 quart dish. Place in shallow pan of water in lowest shelf of oven for 1 hour and 20 minutes. DO NOT OVERBAKE. Remove from water & cool completely on wire rack. Top becomes crusty as pudding cools. Top with ice cream.

Preston's Ice Cream Pie

1	stick butter, melted	½	cup pecans, chopped
1	cup flour	1	quart vanilla ice cream
¼	cup brown sugar, firmly packed	1	can or jar (or your favorite recipe for) hot fudge sauce

Mix melted butter, flour, brown sugar and pecans. Press into bottom and slightly up sides of 2 pie plates (9" size). Bake at 300° until brown, about 15 minutes. Cool completely. Fill one crust with ice cream. Crumble the other crust on top. Cover pie and freeze. When ready, slice and pour hot sauce on top. A man's favorite.

Grandma Larson's Pineapple Ice Box Pudding

1	cup sugar	2	eggs, beaten well
1	small can crushed pineapple, juice also	½	cup butter, soft
1	cup pecans, chopped	½	pint whipped cream
		1	box vanilla wafers

Cream butter & sugar. Add well beaten eggs, pineapple and pecans. Line bottom of 8x12" pan or glass dish with vanilla wafers. Spread wafers with thin layer of pineapple mixture. Continue layers. Top layer should be vanilla wafers. (Three layers of wafers, two layers of pineapple mixture.) Cover and refrigerate overnight. Cut into squares and top each with whipped cream before serving.

Fabulous Fudge Nut Pudding

3	eggs	1	cup pecans, chopped
1½	cups sugar	8	ounces semi-sweet chocolate,
¾	cup flour		melted
¾	cup butter, melted & cooled		

Preheat oven to 350°. In a mixing bowl or saucepan, beat eggs, sugar & flour together until fluffy. Add butter & pecans and pour into a greased 8" square pan. Pour the melted chocolate over the batter & swirl through with a knife. Bake for about 30 minutes or until done.

Kiki's Layered Chocolate Dessert

Layer One:
- 1   stick butter, softened
- 1   cup flour
-      Dash of salt
- 1   cup nuts, chopped

Combine all ingredients and press thinly into a 13x9x2" pan. Bake 20 minutes at 350° until slightly brown. Cool completely.

Layer Two:
- 1   8-ounce package cream cheese, softened
- 1   cup powdered sugar
- 1   cup Cool Whip

Cream above ingredients together & add to top of Layer One.

Layer Three:
- 2   small packages instant chocolate pudding
- 3½   cups milk

Mix together & beat 3 minutes. Pour over Layer Two.

Layer Four:
Top with remaining Cool Whip. Cover & refrigerate 3 hours or overnight.

Cookies & Candies

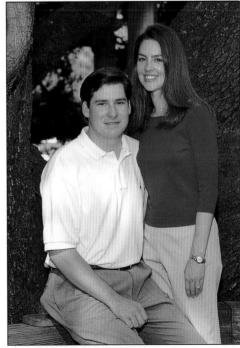

Cookies & Candies

Preceding Page: The Whilden Family
Top row, left to right: The Magness Family–Bobby, Jay, Lisa, John, & Mary Elizabeth.
The Halverson Family–Binford, Margie, Bin, & Whilden.
Robert Whilden III and Carol Grothues.

Toffee Squares

Graham cracker squares, enough to cover bottom of pan (4 across cover the pan)
1 cup butter
1 cup light brown sugar
1 cup pecans, ground
1 teaspoon vanilla extract

Line a pan (at least 10x15") with foil on bottom & sides. Line with separated rectangle graham crackers (not crumbs) placed side-by-side. Combine butter, sugar, vanilla, & nuts and simmer for 3 minutes. Pour mixture quickly over the crackers and bake in a 350° preheated oven for 10-12 minutes.

Note: For variety, when hot from the oven pour chocolate chips over the top and spread as they melt.

Chocolate Chip Cookies

1 cup butter
1 cup brown sugar
1 cup granulated sugar
2 eggs
1 teaspoon vanilla
2 cups flour
2-2¼ cups oatmeal, ground
½ teaspoon salt
1 teaspoon baking powder
1 teaspoon baking soda
12 ounces chocolate chips
4-ounce bar chocolate, finely grated
1½ cups walnuts, chopped

Soften butter & mix with sugar. Beat in eggs & vanilla. Mix in the dry ingredients. The oatmeal has to be ground in a blender or a food processor. The chocolate also has to be grated using a grater of some kind (I use a parmesan cheese grater. this is the most painful part and the ideal job for spouses who offer to help). Preheat the oven to 375°. Drop cookies onto a greased cookie sheet and bake for 10-12 minutes. I check after 7-8 minutes and take them out when it looks like those gourmet cookies you yearn for in shopping malls.

Note: I have also done a short cut when I do this with the children. I bypass the grated chocolate & use M&M chips for fun & skip the nuts. This appears to be a popular modified version for our crew.

Kendall's Sugar Cookies

1	stick butter		1	cup flour, sifted
1	egg		5	teaspoons vanilla
1	cup granulated sugar		1	teaspoon baking soda

I always double this recipe when I make it. Sometimes I double the vanilla & sometimes I use only the 5 teaspoons. Try it both ways. Be sure to take butter and eggs out early to get to room temperature. Cream butter & sugar together. Add egg, flour & vanilla. Drop from teaspoon onto greased cookie sheet. These cookies come out thin & crisp.

Note: Place cookies on waxed paper to cool. Sprinkle with just a bit of sugar to decorate.

Janet's Chocolate Chip Sand Tarts

1	cup butter		1	egg
⅛	teaspoon salt		2	cups flour, sifted
1	teaspoon vanilla extract		1	6-ounce package chocolate chips
½	teaspoon almond extract			
1¼	cups granulated sugar			

Combine the butter, salt, vanilla & almond extract. Blend well. Beat in sugar gradually. Beat in egg. Stir in flour & add chocolate chips. Drop by teaspoonfuls on ungreased cookie sheet. Bake at 350° for 10-12 minutes or until edges get brown. The tops will stay white.

Jane's Chocolate Bark

6	squares semi-sweet chocolate	1½	cups walnuts or pecans, chopped
6	squares white chocolate		

Melt chocolate in separate pan over low heat, stirring constantly. Stir ¾ cup nuts in each pan. Line cookie sheet or 9x13" pan (I prefer using a baking dish so chocolate won't run out) with waxed paper. Alternately spoon melted chocolates onto waxed paper. Swirl chocolates together with knife to marbelize. Refrigerate 1 hour or until firm. Makes one pound. Break into pieces, serve & watch disappear.

Morgan's Chocolate Brownies

½	cup granulated sugar	1	cup flour, sifted
½	cup corn syrup	¼	teaspoon salt
½	cup unsalted butter	1	teaspoon baking powder
2	eggs	1	12-ounce package semi-sweet chocolate chips
1	teaspoon vanilla		
6	tablespoons cocoa	½	cup chopped nuts, optional

In a large bowl, combine sugar, corn syrup and butter and beat well. Add one egg at a time and beat well after each addition. Continue beating until batter becomes fluffy & light. Stir in vanilla & cocoa & beat again. In a medium bowl, sift together dry ingredients. Mix together with the chocolate mixture. Gently fold in chocolate morsels. Add nuts (if desired). Pour mixture into greased 8x12x2" baking dish. Bake at 350° for 30-40 minutes. Cut while warm & cool on rack.

Kelsey's Gingermen

¼	cup butter	1	teaspoon soda
½	cup sugar, white and/or brown	½	teaspoon cinnamon
½	cup dark molasses	¾	teaspoon ginger
5	tablespoons water	¼	teaspoon cloves
3½	cups flour	½	teaspoon salt

Cream butter & sugar. Add molasses & beat. Sift together dry ingredients. Sift again. Add dry ingredients to creamed mixture in 3 or 4 parts. Alternate with water (may need a little more water). This will be very stiff, so work with your hands. Roll out to desired thickness & cut with cookie cutter. Preheat 350° oven. Bake for 8-10 minutes depending on thickness of cookies. Promptly remove from pan and cool.

Note: Decorate with raisins, nuts & chips before baking. To ice them, mix cup powdered sugar with a few drops of water & food coloring. Apply with a toothpick. Make several batches of icing for more decorative effect.

Randa's Praline Brownies

1	box brownie mix	1	teaspoon vanilla or almond extract
¾	cup pecans or almonds, chopped		
		3	tablespoons margarine, melted
		¾	cup light brown sugar

Prepare brownies according to package directions & add extract flavoring. Place on a greased 9x13x2" pan. Combine nuts & brown sugar in separate bowl. Sprinkle over batter. Bake for 25 minutes at 350°.

Galen's Chocolate Chip Cookies

1	stick butter, softened		1	teaspoon baking soda
1	cup vegetable oil		1	teaspoon cream of tartar
1	cup brown sugar, packed		1	cup regular oats, uncooked
1	cup granulated sugar		1	cup Rice Krispies cereal
1	egg		1	16-ounce package semi-sweet
2	teaspoons vanilla			chocolate chips
3½	cups flour		¾	cup nuts, chopped (optional)
1	teaspoon salt			

Cream butter & oil. Add sugar & beat well. Add egg & vanilla. In a separate bowl sift flour, baking soda, salt & cream of tartar. Add to creamed mixture, mixing well. With a spoon, stir in oats, cereal, chocolate chips & nuts. Drop dough on ungreased cookie sheet & bake at 375° for 10-12 minutes until light brown on top. Cool on cookie sheet at least 3 minutes, then remove to wire racks. Cool completely. Makes 8-12 dozen depending on size of each cookie.

Note: Semi-sweet chips can be substituted with a mix of milk chocolate & white chocolate.

Chubby's Pralines

1	cup milk		1	tablespoon vanilla
2	cups sugar		¼	stick butter
½	teaspoon salt		½-1	cup pecans, chopped

Bring sugar & milk to a boil; boil over medium heat, stirring occasionally, until mixture forms a hard ball in a cup of cold water. Remove from heat & add salt, butter, & vanilla. Beat until it becomes white & creamy. Add pecans. When it looks thick enough to turn hard, put spoonfuls of mixture onto waxed paper.

Note: This was my father's old Louisiana praline recipe and it is the best candy you will ever eat!

Real Chocolate Brownies Rienzi

2	squares unsweetened chocolate
⅓	cup butter
1	cup granulated sugar
⅔	cup flour
½	cup nuts, chopped (optional)
2	eggs
½	teaspoon baking powder
¼	teaspoon salt
1	teaspoon vanilla

Brownie Icing:

2	cups granulated sugar
¼	teaspoon salt
2	ounces unsweetened chocolate
2	tablespoons corn syrup, light
⅔	cup milk
1	tablespoon butter
1	teaspoon vanilla

Melt chocolate in butter on very low heat. Combine flour, salt, baking powder & sugar. Add chocolate to dry ingredients. Add eggs & vanilla, beating lightly. Pour into an 11x7" non-stick pan. bake at 350°. Watch mixture & when it begins to bubble, stir with a fork. Stir several times. Bake for 25 minutes. Ice with fudge icing below.

Icing: Melt chocolate on low heat. Add sugar, salt, corn syrup & milk to saucepan. Mix well & boil for 5-10 minutes on medium heat, stirring constantly. Add butter and vanilla. Beat well until thick enough to pour on brownies.

Bobby & Jay's S'Mores

1	box graham crackers
1	package Hershey Chocolate Kisses

1	package large marshmallows

On a microwaveable plate, place a square shaped graham cracker, 1 chocolate Kiss and 1 large marshmallow, 1 more graham cracker square. Heat for 10-15 seconds or until chocolate is melted.

Margaret Fraser's Peanut Butter Sandies

¾ cup peanut butter, smooth
½ cup vegetable oil
½ cup packed brown sugar
1 teaspoon vanilla
1 egg

1½ cups flour
2 teaspoons baking powder
½ teaspoon baking soda
½ cup blender chopped pecans, extra fine

Cream peanut butter, oil, sugar, vanilla and egg. Add remaining ingredients and mix. Form moon shaped cookies. Bake on greased cookie sheet at 350° for about 12-15 minutes. Roll each warm cookie in powdered sugar. Makes 3-3½ dozen cookies.

Robert's Easy Ice Box Cinnamon Cookies

Sift together and set aside:
3½ cups flour
1 teaspoon baking soda
2 tablespoons cinnamon
¼ teaspoon salt

1 cup Crisco
1 cup brown sugar
1 cup white sugar
2 eggs
1 cup pecans, chopped

Cream Crisco and sugar, add beaten eggs. Then add sifted ingredients. Add nuts. Shape dough into rolls. Roll up in waxed paper and store in refrigerator 12 hours. Slice ¼" thick and place on ungreased cookie sheet. Bake at 350° for 7-10 minutes.

Whilden's Chocolate Chip Brownies

1	cup butter	1½	cups all purpose flour
4	ounces unsweetened chocolate	⅛	teaspoon salt
2	cups sugar	2	cups pecans, chopped
4	large eggs, beaten	6	ounces semi-sweet chocolate
2	teaspoons pure vanilla extract		chips

Melt butter and chocolate in top of double boiler over simmering water. Cool to room temperature. In large mixing bowl, cream sugar, eggs and vanilla; blend in chocolate mixture. Add flour and salt; mix well. Stir in pecans and chocolate chips. Spread batter into greased and floured 9x13" pan. Bake at 350° for 25-30 minutes. Cool. Frost with Cream Cheese Frosting. Makes 24 brownies.

Cream Cheese Frosting:

3	ounces cream cheese, softened
6	tablespoons butter, softened
1	tablespoon whole milk
1	teaspoon pure vanilla extract
3	cups powdered sugar

In medium bowl, beat cream cheese until soft. Add butter, mixing until smooth. Stir in milk and vanilla. Gradually add powdered sugar, beat until smooth and spread onto cooled brownies.

Harrison's Snicker Doodles

1	cup butter, room temperature	2	teaspoons cream of tartar
2	cups granulated sugar	2	teaspoons baking soda
2	eggs, beaten to blend	½	teaspoon salt
2¾	cups flour, all purpose	1-2	teaspoons cinnamon

Grease baking sheet, preheat oven to 400° & position rack in upper third of oven. Cream butter with 1½ cups sugar in large bowl on low speed. Add eggs & continue beating 1 minute. Sift flour, cream of tartar, baking soda & salt in medium bowl. Stir into egg mixture. Refrigerate dough 30 minutes. Mix remaining ½ cup of sugar & cinnamon in shallow dish. Shape dough into 1" balls & roll in sugar mixture. Arrange on baking sheet. Bake until golden, 6½-8 minutes for a chewy cookie, 10 minutes for a crunchy one.

Kay's Chocolate Cookies

1	6-ounce package chocolate chips	½	teaspoon salt
⅔	cup condensed milk	1	cup chopped pecans
1	teaspoon vanilla		

Melt chocolate chips and condensed milk in double boiler. Add other ingredients. Drop by spoonfuls on greased cookie sheet. Bake 10 minutes in 350° oven.

Cy's Sugar Cookies

1	cup butter	1	teaspoon salt
1	cup sugar	1	teaspoon vanilla
2	eggs		Pecan halves
2	cups flour		

Mix all ingredients except pecan halves. Drop by teaspoonfuls on greased cookie sheet. Press 1 pecan half into each mound of dough. Bake in 350° oven about 7 minutes, until edges are brown.

Note: Kids love to substitute M&M's for the pecans.

Dottie B's Oatmeal Cookies

¾	cup shortening	1	teaspoon cinnamon	
1	cup sugar		a little soda dissolved in 2	
2	eggs		tablespoons water	
1	cup flour	2	cups oatmeal	
1	teaspoon nutmeg	1	cup chopped nuts	

Preheat oven to 350°. Cream sugar and shortening. Add beaten eggs. Then add flour, water, oatmeal, spices and nuts. Drop dough by teaspoonfuls on a greased cookie sheet. Sprinkle with sugar, and bake at 350° until they begin to brown.

Scottie's Best Pralines

3	cups broken pecan pieces	3	tablespoons white Karo syrup
4	regular marshmallows, cut	½	cup, Half & Half cream
1	teaspoon almond extract		Pinch of salt
1½	cups sugar		
½	cup dark brown sugar		

Cook sugars, Karo, cream and salt to form softball when dropped in cold water. Add marshmallows & extract. When marshmallows have melted add pecans. Beat together & pour by teaspoons onto foil or waxed paper. Cool completely and remove. They will then be firm.

Adelaide & Emmy's *Chachi*
Chachi One

2	sticks butter	¼	teaspoon salt
1	12-ounce package semi-sweet chocolate chips	1	13-ounce can evaporated milk
1	6-ounce package semi-sweet chocolate chips	4½	cups sugar
		2	teaspoons vanilla
1	7½-ounce jar marshmallow cream	2	cups pecans, chopped

Put cut up butter, chocolate & marshmallows in a large mixing bowl. Bring milk, sugar & salt to a boil. Bring to soft-boil stage (235°), stirring constantly. Pour into bowl & beat all together. Stir in vanilla & nuts. Pour into buttered 9x13" pan & let cool. Cut into desired piece sizes.

Chachi Two

1	12-ounce package semi-sweet chocolate chips	1	tablespoon water
		1	teaspoon vanilla
⅔	cup sweetened condensed milk	½	cup pecan, chopped

Melt chocolate over hot water or in microwave. Stir in milk, water & vanilla. When very smooth add pecans. Spread into buttered 9x5x3" loaf pan. Chill until firm. Cut into squares, or may be rolled into balls.

Mary's Pecan Tassies

2	sticks butter, +2 tablespoons		½	teaspoon vanilla
2	3-ounce packages cream cheese		1½	cup brown sugar
			1½	cups pecans
2	eggs			

Soften 2 sticks butter in mixing bowl. Add cream cheese & work with spoon until soft & creamy. Add butter in fourths, blending thoroughly after each addition. Work with fingers to smooth blended dough. If desired, refrigerate dough for easier shaping. Pinch off small pieces of dough & shape into balls about 1¼" in diameter. Put each ball in cup of 1¾" muffin pans. With thumb press dough against bottom & sides, lining up evenly. *Pecan Filling:* Beat eggs only enough to mix yolk with white. Add brown sugar gradually, beating well after each addition. Add 2 tablespoons melted butter, dash of salt & vanilla. Mix well. Sprinkle pecans into lined muffin cups, using ½ the nuts, filling cups not quite full then sprinkle with remaining nuts. Bake at 350° for 15-17 minutes. Reduce heat to 250° & bake 10 minutes longer or until filling is set & firm. Cool. Carefully remove from pans to rack. Makes 4 dozen.

Roadrunner's Texas Pecan Brittle

1	cup sugar		1	tablespoons butter
½	cup light corn syrup		1	teaspoon vanilla
⅛	teaspoon salt		1	teaspoon baking soda
1-1½	cups pecans, halved & quartered			

Combine sugar, syrup & salt in 2 quart casserole or mixing bowl. Microwave on high for 5 minutes. Stir in pecans. Microwave for 3-4 minutes. Stir in butter, vanilla & soda until light & foaming. Spread ¼" thick on large buttered cookie sheet. Makes 1 pound.

Whilden Family Sugar Cookies

⅔ cup soft butter
¾ cup sugar
1 egg
¾ teaspoon vanilla
¼ teaspoon almond extract

2 cups flour
1½ teaspoon baking powder
¼ teaspoon salt
4 teaspoons milk

Cream butter & sugar; add egg, and vanilla and beat well. Combine baking soda & salt and stir into sugar mixture. Divide dough into 2 parts. Chill 1 hour. Roll to ⅛" thickness on floured board and cut with favorite cookie cutter. Bake on ungreased cookie sheet 8-10 minutes in 375° oven.

Margaret Stewart's Oatmeal Cookies

3 cups light brown sugar
1 cup Crisco shortening, melted
2 eggs, beaten
1 cup coconut
4 cups oatmeal, uncooked
2 cups flour, sifted

½ teaspoon salt
½ teaspoon baking powder
1 teaspoon soda
½ teaspoon nutmeg
½ teaspoon cinnamon

Mix all ingredients & drop from spoon onto ungreased sheet pan. Bake 350° for 10 minutes.

Lois' Brown Sugar Cookies

2	sticks butter	1½	cups flour, sifted
1	box brown sugar	1	teaspoon vanilla
2	eggs, beaten	1	cup pecans, chopped
¼	teaspoon salt		

Melt butter, add brown sugar. Stir and melt together. Cool 15 minutes. Add eggs, salt, flour, vanilla, and pecans. Bake in floured 9x12" pan at 350° for about 35-40 minutes. Cool slightly before cutting.

Mary's Lemon Squares

1   cup flour, sifted
½   cup butter

Mix well & pat thinly onto pan. Bake at 325° for 10 minutes.

Mix together:
½   cup moist coconut
1½ cup brown sugar
1   cup pecans, chopped
2   tablespoons flour
¼   teaspoon baking powder
½   teaspoon salt
2   eggs, beaten
1   teaspoon vanilla
2   tablespoons lemon juice

Pour this mixture over slightly baked dough. Bake 25-30 minutes at 325°. Cool & spread with frosting.

Frosting:
1¼ cups powdered sugar
3   tablespoons butter

Mix together & moisten with lemon juice; just enough to spread over mixture.

Juan's Chocolate Chip Toffee Bars

2 ⅓	cups flour, all-purpose		1	cup nuts, coarsely chopped
⅔	cup light brown sugar, firmly packed		1	14-ounce can Eagle Brand sweetened condensed milk (original, low-fat or fat-free)
¾	cup margarine or butter		1	10-ounce package toffee bits
1	egg, slightly beaten			
1	12-ounce package semi-sweet chocolate chips			

Preheat oven to 350°. In large bowl, sift together flour & sugar. Cut in margarine until mixture resembles coarse crumbs. Add egg; mix well. Stir in 1½ cups chocolate chips & the cup of nuts. Reserve 1½ cups crumb mixture. Press remaining crumb mixture onto bottom of 13x9" greased baking pan. Bake 10 minutes. Pour Eagle Brand evenly over crust; top with 1½ cups toffee bits. Sprinkle reserved crumb mixture & remaining chips over top. Bake 25-30 minutes or until golden brown. Sprinkle with remaining toffee bits. Cool completely. Cut into bars. Makes about 36 bars.

Binford's Brown Sugar Cookies

1	cup light brown sugar		1½	cups pecans, chopped
1	egg white		1	teaspoon vanilla

Beat egg white until stiff. Add sugar, nuts & vanilla. Drop from spoon onto greased flat pan, leaving room to spread. Cook in 325° oven until crisp, about 10 minutes.

Index

D

E

F

Q

R

S

T

V

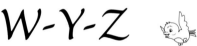

W-Y-Z

Order Forms

Please send me .... copies of the ***Out of the Nest–Cuckoo 2000*** cookbook at $20.00 each (*please add $3.50 for postage & handling; Texas residents add $1.65 for tax*).

Enclosed is $ ....

Name ....

Address ....

City .... State .... Zip ....

Make check payable to: ***Out of the Nest, Inc.***
c/o Reckling
5142 Green Tree
Houston, Texas 77056-1406

Please send me .... copies of the ***Out of the Nest–Cuckoo 2000*** cookbook at $20.00 each (*please add $3.50 for postage & handling; Texas residents add $1.65 for tax*).

Enclosed is $ ....

Name ....

Address ....

City .... State .... Zip ....

Make check payable to: ***Out of the Nest, Inc.***
c/o Reckling
5142 Green Tree
Houston, Texas 77056-1406

Kitchen Closed -
These old birds have had it!